Introduction of Cosmetology Exam

The National-Interstate Council of State Boards of Cosmetology offers cosmetology exam and it is necessary to obtain a license or certification in the majority of states. The cosmetology exam consists of two parts that assess a cosmetologist's knowledge and skill in a range of topics relevant to their line of work. The exam consists of a written multiple-choice test and a hands-on practical test, although some states do not require the practical portion. Professionals and students can use online tools to assist them study for the examination by creating practice questions and flashcards.

The Cosmetology exam consist four main domains:

1. Scientific Concepts

This domain covers infection control, safety practices, and scientific foundations. It includes understanding disease transmission, infection control levels, and government regulations. Candidates must grasp human anatomy, product chemistry, and their effects, including pH scales, chemical interactions, and reactions to ensure safe and effective practices.

2. Hair Care and Services

Cosmetology exam encompasses hair care and services, covering client consultation and assessment, tools used in hair care, shampooing, conditioning, scalp treatments, and hair design techniques including cutting, styling, and enhancements like extensions. It also includes chemical services such as coloring, lightening, relaxing, and texturizing, emphasizing safety, procedures, and principles across these practices.

3. Skin Care and Services

This domain centers on skin care, including client assessment, tools, infection control, and safe practices. It covers facial procedures, hair removal, makeup, and emphasizes safety measures.

4. Nail Care and Services

This domain assesses nail conditions, tools, and safe practices. It covers manicures, pedicures, and applying/removing nail enhancements like tips and acrylics.

About the Author

The Author is cosmetologist himself and have experience is cosmetology field from many years. He is very passionate to his field and got many success in USA by achieving the certified certifications in the field of cosmetology and Author educate lots of student in cosmetology field.

The author write these 4 PTS with the help of other cosmetologist and senior salon worker to check all the key point used in cosmetology exam.

Author studies cosmetology exam by himself with the help of official authority of cosmetology exam and given references. All the questions in this cosmetology exam are based on official domain content and real life exam, by reading these 4 PTS you are able to get maximum knowledge to pass the exam, however as author himself is also a human so some mistake is possible, we are working day and night to improve day by day.

If you found any mistake please email us by scanning the QR code below:

Cosmetology Exam Practice Test-1

Q1. While using a dirty salon tools and equipment on clients, what are its disadvantage?

(A) Trendy hairstyles

(B) Harm and infection

(C) Positive reviews

(D) Increased profits

Q2. A bacteria that grows and reproduces is adapted to warm and moist conditions, which bacterial phase is involved?

(A) Dormant stage

(B) Inactive stage

(C) Active stage

(D) Mitotic stage

Q3. Which bacterial life stage contains spores that can tolerate drought and unfavorable temperatures?

a) Inactive stage

b) Spore-forming stage

c) Dormant stage

d) Reproductive stage

Q4. To deal with disinfectants, what is an important safety tip?

(A) Pouring over hands

(B) Mixing with water first

(C) Using bare hands

(D) Direct skin contact

Q5. When dealing with disinfectants in cosmetology. Which safety precaution is important?

(A) Wear gloves and safety glasses

(B) Apply disinfectant directly to the skin

(C) Mix water into the disinfectant

(D) Store disinfectants within reach of children

Q6. In cosmetology, how should disinfectants be mixed?

(A) Add water to disinfectant

(B) Mix with other chemicals first

(C) Mix according to label instructions

(D) Pour disinfectant over hands

Q7. While using multi use tools, how can cosmetologists effectively prevent cross contamination?

(A) Storing tools in a humid environment

(B) Using tools without cleaning between clients

(C) Cleaning and disinfecting tools between clients

(D) Rinsing tools with lukewarm water

Q8. In a cosmetology setting what significant advantage does the use of single use items offer?

(A) Simplifying tool maintenance procedures

(B) Reducing salon waste and environmental impact

(C) Eliminating the need for sanitation measures

(D) Maximizing the lifespan of tools

Q9. In cosmetology practice what role do Material Safety Data sheets (MSDS) play?

(A) Provide styling tips

(B) Ensure client satisfaction

(C) Communicate hazards and precautions

(D) Offer product discounts

Q10. In regulating disinfectants used in salons, what main purpose does the Environmental Protection Agency have?

(A) Setting fashion trends

(B) Licensing and ensuring the safety of disinfectants

(C) Regulating salon hours

(D) Approving cosmetic ingredients

Q11. In the salon for discarding disposable contaminated objects what kind of method is recommended?

(A) Single-bagging

(B) Triple-bagging

(C) Double-bagging

(D) Placing directly in the trash bin

Q12. After stopping the service what should a cosmetologist do immediately during a blood exposure incident?

(A) Apply an antiseptic with bare hands.

(B) Dispose of contaminated items in a single bag.

(C) Clean the injured area without using gloves.

(D) Wear gloves to protect against blood contact.

Q13. During cosmetology procedures, what step should a practitioner take before returning to a service after sustaining a cut?

(A) Cleaning all affected surface areas

(B) Disinfecting the work surface

(C) Sealing contaminated items in double bags

(D) Applying an antiseptic with an applicator

Q14. To ensure the safety of the client what measure should a cosmetologist prioritize in the event of a blood exposure?

(A) Implementing a strict quarantine protocol

(B) Utilizing a specialized biohazard containment unit

(C) Offering prompt and appropriate wound care

(D) Disposing of contaminated implements in a marked box

Q15. What is a characteristic feature of vellus hair, as per knowledge of cosmetology?

(A) Coarse and pigmented

(B) Absence of a medulla

(C) Typically found on the scalp

(D) Presence on the legs and arms

Q16. What is the main component of the outermost layer of the epidermis, which is continually shed and replaced?

(A) Keratin

(B) Melanin

(C) Sebum

(D) Collagen

Q17. The specialized ligaments near the edges of the nail bed and matrix bed serve to:

(A) Produce nail cells

(B) Hold the nail in place

(C) Increase nail thickness

(D) Create the nail grooves

Q18. Which disorder can cause hair to break off and lead to uneven lengths?

(A) Trichorrhexis nodosa

(B) Telogen effluvium

(C) Scabies

(D) Seborrheic dermatitis

Q19. In both men and women, which disorder can cause gradual hair thinning due to hair thinning?

(A) Alopecia areata

(B) Telogen effluvium

(C) Androgenetic alopecia

(D) Traction alopecia

Q20. Which skin disorder causes the hips, thighs, and buttocks to seem dimpled?

(A) Rosacea

(B) Hyperpigmentation

(C) Cellulite

(D) Stretch marks

Q21. Due to dry skin or small cuts, which condition contains the living skin around the nail plate splitting and tearing?

(A) Hangnail

(B) Onychophagy

(C) Onychia

(D) Ridges

Q22. What is the main function of the facial nerve divisions, as per cosmetology knowledge?

(A) Control of neck muscles

(B) Control of facial expression muscles

(C) Control of scalp muscles

(D) Control of arm muscles

Q23. The muscles behind the ear, at the base of the skull, are affected by which nerve:

(A) Temporal nerve

(B) Posterior auricular nerve

(C) Marginal mandibular nerve

(D) Buccal nerve

Q24. By which sense organs, sensory nerves transmit impulses:

(A) Muscles

(B) Glands

(C) Brain

(D) Spinal cord

Q25. What role does blood circulation play to impact skin elasticity?

(A) Influences skin elasticity

(B) Determines hair thickness

(C) Provides nutrients to nails

(D) Regulates makeup application

Q26. For having spa treatments, why is the knowledge of the circulatory system important?

(A) Helps in hair coloring techniques

(B) Prevents allergic reactions to makeup

(C) Minimizes risks during massages

(D) Determines skin exfoliation frequency

Q27. What bone contributes in forming an inner corner of the eye?

(A) Nasal bone

(B) Lacrimal bone

(C) Zygomatic bone

(D) Maxilla bone

Q28. In the formation of the elbow joint by the articulation, which bone joins with the humerus?

(A) Ulna

(B) Radius

(C) Carpals

(D) Metacarpals

Q29. Concerning the impact on hair characteristics, what is the key role of alkalis in cosmetology products?

(A) Harden the hair

(B) Soften and swell hair

(C) Promote combustion

(D) Increase acidity

Q30. In cosmetology, what is the main characteristic of organic substances?

(A) Ability to burn

(B) Natural and healthy

(C) Inorganic composition

(D) Lack of carbon content

Q31. From the following options, what is the comparison of pH of pure water to the average pH of hair and skin?

(A) More acidic

(B) More alkaline

(C) Neutral

(D) Highly volatile

Q32. Regarding hair color products, shampoos, chemical hair texturizers, and styling aids. Considering the following options which field of chemistry focuses on substances containing carbon?

(A) Inorganic chemistry

(B) Analytical chemistry

(C) Organic chemistry

(D) Physical chemistry

Q33. Due to hidden oil, which type of emulsion does not feel as greasy?

(A) Oil-in-water

(B) Water-in-oil

(C) Gel-in-water

(D) Suspension

Q34: In hair products, what is the primary function of ammonium hydroxide?

(A) Create exothermic reactions

(B) Raise the pH

(C) Form stable emulsions

(D) Act as a surfactant

Q35. When adding a preservative to a cosmetic product with hair, which of the following aspect is crucial?

(A) pH range effectiveness

(B) Fragrance compatibility

(C) Color stability

(D) Texture enhancement

Q36. When evaluating the pH of non-aqueous products, especially those used on hair or skin with water, which of the following techniques are utilized?

(A) Mix with oil

(B) Mix with alcohol

(C) Mix with distilled water

(D) Mix with vinegar

Q37. Concerning its functional purpose in skincare products, what role does benzophenone serve?

(A) Enhance fragrance

(B) Prevent UV degradation

(C) Provide color

(D) Improve texture

Q38. In the context of safeguarding the skin from harmful sun exposure, what is the main function of oxybenzone in sun protection products?

(A) Enhance fragrance for a pleasant scent

(B) Actively absorb and mitigate UV rays to prevent skin damage

(C) Contribute color variations for product aesthetics

(D) Supply moisture to keep the skin hydrated

Q39. How can hair cause to become dry and brittle?

(A) Proper diet

(B) Well-functioning glands

(C) Lack of protein and vitamins

(D) Regular hair brushing

Q40. For return services, why it is essential to quick consultation?

(A) To discuss payment

(B) To prevent misunderstandings

(C) To schedule future appointments

(D) To update client records

Q41. In client care, what role does knowledge of anatomy play for cosmetologists?

(A) Enhances artistic skills

(B) Recommends specific hairstyles

(C) Guides medical treatments

(D) Determines suitable services

Q42. In the context of ingrown hairs, which layer of skin is primarily affected by the inflammatory obstruction?

(A) Epidermis

(B) Dermis

(C) Hypodermis

(D) Papillary layer

Q43. What distinguishes total contraindications from relative contraindications. When assessing contraindications?

(A) Severity

(B) Duration

(C) Frequency

(D) Progression

Q44. Before providing treatment, what step can a cosmetologist take for clients with skin conditions?

(A) Ignore the condition

(B) Request a medical note

(C) Use stronger products

(D) Provide treatment without inquiry

Q45. For hair coloring services, why preview testing is essential?

(A) To enhance scalp health

(B) To evaluate styling preferences

(C) To assess pre-treatment needs

(D) To choose the right shampoo

Q46. In the context abnormal diffuse hair loss during the growth phase. When support of physician crucial for patients?

(A) Trichorrhexis nodosa

(B) Telogen effluvium

(C) Androgenetic alopecia

(D) Anagen effluvium

Q47. What area of the scalp is commonly affected in female pattern hair loss, leading to a "Christmas Tree" pattern?

(A) Frontal hairline

(B) Vertex crown

(C) Occipital region

(D) Parietal region

Q48. During the confirming of the diagnosis, what is the key scalp pathology finding in lichen planopilaris?

(A) Sebaceous gland stimulation

(B) Papilla inflammation

(C) Lymphocytic infiltrate

(D) Hair follicle hyperactivity

Q49. Commonly, which therapy is used for Central Centrifugal Cicatricial Alopecia and including the application of substance like corticosteroids doxycycline, and intralesional injections?

(A) Phototherapy

(B) Aromatherapy

(C) Hot Oil Treatment

(D) Topical Corticosteroids

Q50. Individuals who haven't undergone a patch test. Why is performing hair care treatments on them prohibited?

(A) Compliance with laws

(B) Treatment protocol

(C) Emergency contact details

(D) Results of treatment

Q51. In cosmetology, what is the purpose of using a rat-tail comb?

(A) Hair teasing

(B) Sectioning hair

(C) Creating curls

(D) Detangling hair

Q52. In a salon setting, what is the key objective of having a shampoo station?

(A) Displaying salon aesthetics

(B) Facilitating hairstyling competitions

(C) Providing a designated area for hair washing

(D) Minimizing salon costs

Q53. What must be done after using a hair roller, and how does it work in styling hair?

(A) Heats and straightens; discard after one use

(B) Curls with heat; store without cleaning

(C) Curls without heat; wipe with a damp cloth

(D) Adds shine; disinfect after each use

Q54. In cosmetology, what is the purpose of using a non-absorbent coverings on chairs, and how it contributes to infection control procedures?

(A) Enhancing client comfort

(B) Preventing contamination

(C) Facilitating easy storage

(D) Minimizing equipment costs

Q55. Why cosmetologists use a hair roller with a blow-dryer in hairstyling?

A) Adds shine to the hair

B) Precision sectioning

C) Creates textured styles

D) Changing hair structure

Q56. In cosmetology settings, how does the use of electric clippers differ from hair irons?

A) Achieving closer cuts

B) Changing hair structure

C) Creating textured styles

D) Wet hair styling

Q57. In cosmetology, why is it necessary to follow MN Rule 2105.0375, subparts 3 and 4 for hair or color brushes?

A) Adds shine to the hair

B) Precision sectioning

C) Ensures proper cleaning and disinfection

D) Achieves closer cuts

Q58. When blow-drying hair, what is the primary purpose of using a vent brush in cosmetology?

(A) Adds shine to the hair

(B) Detangles wet hair

(C) Accelerates drying time

(D) Precision parting

Q59. In cosmetology setting, what is the primary function of a linen towel during a hair color application?

(A) Adds comfort to the client

(B) Enhances hair color absorption

(C) Ensures hygiene and safety

(D) Creates volume in hairstyles

Q60. Which of the following prevents excessive current from passing through a circuit in electrical equipment?

(A) Circuit breaker

(B) Grounding

(C) Fuse

(D) Two-prong plug

Q61. In cosmetology settings, why it is necessary to wear gloves when handling chemical products?

(A) To enhance creativity

(B) To prevent contamination

(C) To showcase professionalism

(D) To create curls in the hair

Q62. What is the purpose of storing wigs in individual clean and disinfected containers?

(A) Enhances styling precision

(B) Prevents tangling

(C) Promotes a hygienic environment

(D) Facilitates easier cleaning

Q63. For reducing dandruff or relieving scalp conditions, which type of shampoo suits best?

(A) Clarifying shampoo

(B) Conditioning shampoo

(C) Medicated shampoo

(D) Balancing shampoo

Q64. What crucial function do humectants perform in hair care, in the realm cosmetology principles?

(A) Absorb moisture or promote moisture retention

(B) Enhance shampoo fragrance

(C) Increase shampoo viscosity

(D) Provide color to the hair

Q65. What are antidandruff products designed to do and how dandruff is caused?

(A) Dryness and itchiness; promote tingling effect

(B) Fungus called malassezia; control dandruff

(C) Environmental factors; soothe the scalp

(D) Hair texture; restore moisture

Q66. While the client is holding the electrode, what method involves applying scalp manipulations during a Scalp treatment?

(A) Indirection method

(B) Kneading technique

(C) Violet ray application

(D) High-frequency treatment

Q67. What crucial role does a protective neck strip serve to fulfill within the draping process?

(A) Enhance client comfort

(B) Create a fashionable look

(C) Protect the client's neck

(D) Improve service precision

Q68. What specifically characterizes the product known as "dry shampoo" in the cosmetology terminology?

(A) Water-based hair treatment

(B) Oil and grease remover

(C) Chemical relaxer

(D) Styling gel

Q69. Which specific classification features tight coils or kinks consistently extending from roots to ends among different type of hair types?

(A) Type 1 - Straight

(B) Type 2 - Wavy

(C) Type 3 - Curly

(D) Type 4 - Coily/Kinky

Q70. Known for its tight curls or coils, what specific challenges are commonly associated with Type 4 hair?

(A) Lack of shine

(B) Curl definition

(C) Frizz, shrinkage, and dryness

(D) Excessive thickness

Q71. In hair design first practicing a new design on a mannequin head, Why is appropriate?

(A) Mannequins are cheaper

(B) It saves time

(C) To avoid design mistakes

(D) Mannequins have better hair

Q72. In the context of hairstyling, which asymmetrical balance involve?

(A) Uneven visual weight

(B) Mirror image halves

(C) Same length on both sides

(D) Equal volume on both sides

Q73. For most hair cutting procedures, which comb is mainly used that has fine and wide teeth?

(A) Wide-tooth comb

(B) Tail comb

(C) Barber comb

(D) Styling or cutting comb

Q74. To produce specific outcomes for clients, what basic skills are important for a cosmetologist?

(A) Hair coloring

(B) Nail art

(C) Hairstyling

(D) Scalp treatments

Q75. When deciding on the perfect hair style for a client, what should a certified cosmetologist do?

(A) Trendiness

(B) Client's age

(C) Lifestyle, face shape, and hair type

(D) Personal preference

Q76. In braiding, what is important to maintain hair health?

(A) Weekly washing

(B) Monthly trimming

(C) Regular styling changes

(D) 6 to 8-week touch-ups

Q77. In cosmetology terms, how can a wig be defined?

(A) Natural hair extension

(B) Head covering made of any material

(C) Artificial hair network covering the head

(D) Temporary hair coloring

Q78. What is the primary disadvantage of the bonding method?

(A) High cost

(B) Long application time

(C) Potential slippage

(D) Limited styling options

Q79. For fine hair, how does the fusion method differ from bonding and tracking?

(A) Less comfortable

(B) More expensive

(C) Creates bulk at the base

(D) Requires certification

Q80. In perm wrapping, what is the function of end papers?

(A) Control hair ends

(B) Add fragrance

(C) Increase heat

(D) Provide color

Q81. In terms of hair strength, which type of side bond contributes significantly to its resilience?

A) Disulfide bonds

B) Salt bonds

C) Hydrogen bonds

D) Peptide bonds

Q82. In what way does the texture of fine hair influence the procedure of hair color processing?

A) Processes color slower

B) Requires more color

C) Reacts unpredictably

D) Processes color faster

Q83. During lightening virgin hair, what is used to protect the scalp during lightening virgin hair?

(A) Plastic clips

(B) Towels

(C) Cotton

(D) Foil

Q84. What is the main objective of utilizing chemical hair relaxing?

(A) Enhance curls

(B) Add volume

(C) Straighten or smooth hair

(D) Introduce waves

Q85. In hair relaxing, what is the primary purpose of hydroxide neutralization?

(A) Increases pH

(B) Deactivates alkaline residues

(C) Rebuilds disulfide bonds

(D) Involves oxidation

Q86. What kind of wave incorporates AMP or MEA and is less favored due to producing weak perms?

(A) Low-pH waves

(B) Thio-free waves

(C) Ammonia-free waves

(D) Exothermic waves

Q87. When applying a perm solution, why is it crucial to wear gloves when applying a perm solution?

(A) Enhance grip on perm rods

(B) Prevents product wastage

(C) Avoids skin contact with chemicals

(D) Speeds up the application process

Q88. What type of hair is typically smooth, glossy, and the least challenging to handle?

(A) Wavy Hair

(B) Coily/Kinky Hair

(C) Straight Hair

(D) Curly Hair

Q89. During a facial treatment, why it is essential for a cosmetologist to utilize a special cleanser for eye makeup removal?

(A) Enhances facial relaxation

(B) Prevents damage to the eyes

(C) Smells better

(D) Reduces cleansing time

Q90. Which of the following skin type has good circulation, tends towards dryness on the cheeks and medium pores?

(A) Oily skin

(B) Dry skin

(C) Combination/normal skin

(D) Sensitive skin

Q91. What is the main reason that clients with head lice should be refused beauty treatment with precautions?

(A) Lice can't be fully eradicated

(B) Contamination is unpreventable

(C) Home treatments are ineffective

(D) Lice can cause allergic reactions

Q92. Which of the following is the primary role of an Electric Facial Epilator?

(A) Removes makeup

(B) Cleanses the face

(C) Pulls out hair from the root

(D) Promotes lymphatic drainage

Q93. What is the main role of increased circulation that benefits the skin during facial steaming?

(A) Causes dryness

(B) Boosts oxygen supply

(C) Promotes acne

(D) Reduces collagen production

Q94. From the given option, what is a key ingredients in effective moisturizers for older, dry skin?

(A) Petroleum jelly

(B) Alcohol

(C) Hydrogen peroxide

(D) Aloe vera

Q95. In a Material Safety Data Sheet (MSDS), which of the following must be included?

(A) Product price

(B) Safe handling procedures

(C) Marketing claims

(D) Expiration date

Q96. Why should a cosmetologist ask about a client's medications, during a consultation?

(A) Determine skincare routine

(B) Identify allergies

(C) Assess skin conditions

(D) Avoid contraindications

Q97. During temporary hair removal, what is the main purpose of applying a moist, warm towel before shaving?

(A) Softening the targeted area

(B) Promoting hair regrowth

(C) Enhancing the shaving cream's fragrance

(D) Reducing irritation

Q98. From the given option, what is the main purpose of contouring and highlighting in makeup application?

(A) Adding color variety

(B) Hiding facial flaws

(C) Enhancing good features

(D) Creating natural looks

Q99. What is the role of high-frequency current that benefit acne-prone skin?

(A) Softening sebum

(B) Germicidal effect

(C) Stimulating blood flow

(D) Creating bold color combinations

Q100. Considering the following options, which factor is important for a comprehensive client analysis before starting a nail service?

(A) Nail art preferences

(B) Understanding nail conditions

(C) Payment options

(D) Salon's location history

Q101. Considering the following options, which nail condition might restrict but not necessarily prevent a nail service?

(A) Severe psoriasis of the nail

(B) Brittle nail syndrome

(C) Nail separation (onycholysis)

(D) Paronychia

Q102. From the following options, which service is best when a client wants a long-lasting manicure for an upcoming vacation?

(A) Basic polish application

(B) Acrylic nail extensions

(C) Gel nail polish

(D) French manicure

Q103. What product or service is the most suitable for a client with nail ridges seeking a smoother nail surface?

(A) Nail buffer

(B) Gel polish application

(C) Acrylic sculpting

(D) Nail oil treatment

Q104. Before performing nail services, why it is essential for cosmetologists to record a client's medical history?

(A) To determine the client's favorite services

(B) To understand the client's occupation

(C) To identify potential contraindications or risks

(D) To assess the client's preferred nail colors

Q105. In melted paraffin or wax, which of the following manicures involves in dipping hands?

(A) French Manicure

(B) Paraffin Manicure

(C) Hot Oil Manicure

(D) Acrylic Manicure

Q106. In a disinfection container, why is the total immersion of implements, including handles are crucial?

(A) Enhances cleaning

(B) Saves disinfectant solution

(C) Fulfills EPA requirements

(D) Speeds up disinfection

Q107. When manicurist has only have one set to use, how should they prepare implements?

(A) Clean and disinfect after use

(B) Use without cleaning

(C) Sterilize before each use

(D) Have at least two complete sets

Q108. In a nail care industry what could be the potential consequence of ignoring ergonomic challenges, according to the text?

(A) Increased efficiency

(B) Decreased client satisfaction

(C) Positive impact on nail art designs

(D) Enhanced nail polish application

Q109. To prevent issues with acrylic nail enhancements, why is regular maintenance crucial?

(A) Enhances color vibrancy

(B) Reduces application time

(C) Prevents lifting and cracking

(D) Adds extra shine

Q110. Considering the options, what is thinned down and removed from the acrylic nail during the process of rebalancing?

(A) Thinning apex, removing polish

(B) Thinning the entire nail, removing cuticle

(C) Thinning the nail, removing the apex

(D) Thinning the free edge, removing polish

Test 1 Answer Key

Q1.

Answer: B

Explanation: In this context, using dirty salon tools and equipment on clients can lead to damage and infection. Which highlights the responsibility of providing safe salon services.

Q2.

Answer: C

Explanation: During the active phase. Bacteria grow and thrive in a warm and moist environment.

Q3.

Answer: B

Explanation: In this context. Some bacteria enter the spore forming stage with sterile heat and cold resistant spores.

Q4.

Answer: D

Explanation: Please make sure to avoid direct skin contact and handle with caution. Because antiseptics can seriously damage the skin.

Q5.

Answer: A

Explanation: When dealing with disinfectants in cosmetology. Please protect yourself by wearing gloves and safety glasses to prevent skin and eye damage.

Q6.

Answer: C

Explanation: In the context of cosmetology. Disinfectants in cosmetology should be mixed according to label instructions for proper effectiveness.

Q7.

Answer: C

Explanation: To prevent cross contamination. Cleaning and disinfection of tools between clients is important.

Q8.

Answer: B

Explanation: Benefiting cosmetology practices environmental impact and salon waste are notably reduced by the single use items.

Q9.

Answer: C

Explanation: Ensuring informed and safe practices MSDSs communicate vital information about hazardous ingredients, safe use and handling procedures.

Q10.

Answer: B

Explanation: By specifying the types for salon use and contributing to infection control practices, the EPA ensures the safety of disinfectants by licensing them.

Q11.

Answer: C

Explanation: For proper disposal, disposable contaminated objects should be double bagged.

Q12.

Answer: D

Explanation: For safety esurience, wearing gloves is very important to prevent direct contact with the client's blood.

Q13.

Answer: D

Explanation: Before resuming a service proper care is ensured by applying antiseptic with an applicator.

Q14.

Answer: C

Explanation: To ensure client's health and safety risks are minimized by prompt and proper wound care.

Q15.

Answer: B

Explanation: Vellus hair is fine, short, and typically does not have a medulla. That is commonly found in "hairless" areas.

Q16.

Answer: A

Explanation: The stratum corneum is made up of cells composed of keratin, which continuously shed and renew the skin's surface.

Q17.

Answer: B

Explanation: These ligaments connect the nail bed and matrix bed to underlying bones, securing the nail.

Q18.

Answer: A

Explanation: Trichorrhexis nodosa can cause hair breakage, and makes uneven lengths along the hair shaft.

Q19.

Answer: C

Explanation: Androgenetic alopecia can cause regular hair thinning during hormonal changes in both men and women.

Q20.

Answer: C

Explanation: Cellulite is caused by fat deposits, which misleads connective tissues under the skin. It causes the body parts to look dimpled.

Q21.

Answer: A

Explanation: Hangnails happens, when the skin around the nail plate splits and tears due to dryness or small cuts.

Q22.

Answer: B

Explanation: The primary role of the facial nerve is to control the muscles, which are responsible for facial expressions.

Q23.

Answer: B

Explanation: The posterior auricular nerve influences the muscles, which are located behind the ear at the base of the skull, affecting their movement and function.

Q24.

Answer: C

Explanation: Sensory nerves transmit messages from sense organs to the brain, in order to help the processing of sensory information.

Q25.

Answer: A

Explanation: Proper blood circulation plays an important role in impacting skin elasticity, which results in firmness and suppleness.

Q26.

Answer: C

Explanation: For spa treatments, knowledge of the circulatory system is very important. Because, it helps in minimizing the risks during massages, and ensures a safer experience for clients.

Q27.

Answer: B

Explanation: The lacrimal bone is responsible, to form the inner corner of the eye and support the tear production.

Q28.

Answer: A

Explanation: The elbow joint is formed from the connection between the humerus and the ulna in the lower arm.

Q29.

Answer: B

Explanation: In cosmetology products like chemical hair relaxers, please note that alkalis like sodium hydroxide soften and swell hair.

Q30.

Answer: A

Explanation: Contrary to the misconception that organic implies natural or healthy, please note that organic substances burn due to their carbon content in cosmetology.

Q31.

Answer: B

Explanation: The pH of pure water is 7 which is 100 times more alkaline than the average pH of hair and skin, which makes it potentially dry.

Q32.

Answer: C

Explanation: In the context of hair color products, shampoos, chemical hair texturizers, and styling aids, organic chemistry focuses on substances containing carbon.

Q33:

Answer: A

Explanation: In the case of emulsions, oil-in-water do not feel as greasy since the oil is "hidden" and water forms the external portion.

Q34:

Answer: B

Explanation: The primary function of ammonium hydroxide is to raise the pH in hair products, enhancing hair product absorption into the hair structure.

Q35.

Answer: A

Explanation: To ensure safety and prevent microbial growth, specific pH range effectiveness is crucial when adding a preservative to a cosmetic product with hair.

Q36.

Answer: C

Explanation: During pH evaluation, pH can be determined by mixing non-aqueous products with distilled water before testing with pH strips.

Q37.

Answer: B

Explanation: Benzophenone serve as a protective agent to preserve the product's effectiveness and integrity against sun-induced damage. Please note that it is employed in skincare products to shield against UV degradation.

Q38.

Answer: B

Explanation: Oxybenzone acts as a shield against sun damage to protect the skin. It actively absorbs and mitigates UV rays to prevent skin damage.

Q39.

Answer: C

Explanation: Dry and brittle hair is caused by insufficient intake of essential proteins and vitamins. It is emphasizing the importance of a nourishing diet.

Q40.

Answer: B

Explanation: Before providing return services quick consultations prevent misunderstandings. This practice also ensures continued client satisfaction.

Q41.

Answer: C

Explanation: The knowledge of anatomy helps cosmetologists address various health issues. If necessary, by recommending medical care for the overall well-being of the client.

Q42.

Answer: A

Explanation: Papules, pustules, and cysts develop due to the inflammatory obstruction primarily affecting the epidermis.

Q43.

Answer: A

Explanation: While total contraindications present a significant risk, relative contraindications may allow treatment with modifications based on the severity of the condition.

Q44.

Answer: B

Explanation: When clients have skin conditions, requesting a medical note ensures safety. It reduces the risk of aggravating their condition during treatment.

Q45.

Answer: C

Explanation: Preview testing is essential to determining whether pre-treatment is necessary to achieve the desired hair color result.

Q46.

Answer: D

Explanation: When facing abnormal diffuse hair loss during the growth phase, particularly in anagen effluvium due to events like chemotherapy, seeking physician support is essential.

Q47.

Answer: A

Explanation: In the frontal one to two-thirds of the scalp, leading to a loss of density. Female pattern hair loss often results in a 'Christmas Tree' pattern.

Q48.

Answer: C

Explanation: During the confirming of the diagnosis, scalp pathology in lichen planopilaris reveals a lymphocytic infiltrate around hair follicles.

Q49.

Answer: D

Explanation: Commonly, topical corticosteroids are used in Central Centrifugal Cicatricial Alopecia therapy, reducing inflammation and preventing diseases progression.

Q50.

Answer: A

Explanation: For legal compliance, performing a patch test at least 24 hours prior is mandatory, especially for hair care treatments.

Q51.

Answer: B

Explanation: Cosmetologists commonly use Rat-tail combs for sectioning hair during different styling processes.

Q52.

Answer: C

Explanation: The main purpose of having a shampoo station in a salon is to provide a designated area for hair washing during salon services.

Q53.

Answer: C

Explanation: Cosmetologists use hair rollers to make hairs curly without heat, and they should be wiped with damp cloth after each use for hygiene and safety purposes.

Q54.

Answer: B

Explanation: In cosmetology, the main purpose of using non-absorbent coverings on chairs is to prevent from contamination, which is a crucial aspect of infection control.

Q55.

Answer: D

Explanation: Hair rollers with a blow-dryer are used in hairstyling because they help in changing hair structure, and provide varied styling options and setting techniques.

Q56.

Answer: B

Explanation: Cosmetologists use hair irons to change the hair structure, providing versatility in styling options compared to electric clippers.

Q57.

Answer: C

Explanation: In cosmetology, the main objective of following MN Rule 2105.0375 is to nsure proper cleaning and disinfection of hair or color brushes, and maintaining hygiene and safety standards.

Q58.

Answer: C

Explanation: During blow-drying hair in cosmetology, vent brushes help accelerate the drying time.

Q59.

Answer: B

Explanation: Cosmetologists use linen towels to enhance hair color absorption during a hair color application.

Q60.

Answer: C

Explanation: A fuse ensures safety in the tool usage, and prevents excessive current in electrical circuits.

Q61.

Answer: B

Explanation: It is necessary to wear gloves when handling chemical products to prevent skin contact with chemical products, ensure safety, and prevent contamination in cosmetology practices.

Q62.

Answer: C

Explanation: The main objective of storing wigs in individual clean and disinfected containers is to maintain a hygienic environment in the salon.

Q63.

Answer: C

Explanation: In reducing dandruff and scalp conditions medicated shampoos have effective ingredients.

Q64.

Answer: A

Explanation: Retention within the hair structure, ensuring optimal hydration, humectants play a vital role by either absorbing moisture of promoting it.

Q65.

Answer: B

Explanation: Malassezia causes dandruff in hair and it is controlled by the antidandruff products who suppresses its growth.

Q66.

Answer: A

Explanation: While client holds the electrode the indirection method involves applying scalp manipulations in a scalp treatment.

Q67.

Answer: C

Explanation: Ensuring a protective barrier, the primary purpose of the neck strip is to safeguard the client's neck from potential irritation or discomfort during draping.

Q68.

Answer: B

Explanation: Functioning without the need of water application, dry shampoo is recognized as an oil and grease remover in cosmetology.

Q69.

Answer: D

Explanation: Defining its distinctive texture, Type 4 Coily/Kinky hair exhibits tight coils or kinks throughout its entire length.

Q70.

Answer: C

Explanation: Requiring special care to maintain moisture and manageability, Type 4 hair is characterized by tight curls or coils, often struggles with challenges like frizz, shrinkage and dryness.

Q71.

Answer: C

Explanation: In this context first practicing a new design on a mannequin head helps avoid mistakes and enhances the creative process.

Q72.

Answer: A

Explanation: In the context of hairstyling. An asymmetrical balance involves unequal volume and length on opposite sides.

Q73.

Answer: D

Explanation: In the above context, for most haircutting procedures. Styling or cutting combs, also known as all-purpose combs, are used.

Q74.

Answer: C

Explanation: To create specific outcomes for clients. A hairstyling is fundamental for creating desired looks and teaching clients and staying current with trends.

Q75.

Answer: C

Explanation: When deciding on the best and flattering hairstyle for a client. Consider lifestyle, face shape and hair type.

Q76.

Answer: D

Explanation: In the context of braiding. A regular touch-ups every 6 to 8 weeks help maintain the hairs healthy integrity and appearance.

Q77.

Answer: C

Explanation: In terms of cosmetology. A wig is defined as an artificial head consisting of woven hair.

Q78.

Answer: C

Explanation: In this context. While bonding is fast there is a certain degree of slippage associated with this method.

Q79.

Answer: C

Explanation: The fusion method for fine hair is different from bonding and tracking. That is why fusion procedures are preferred for fine hair. Because bonding and tracking can create bulk at the base.

Q80.

Answer: A

Explanation: End papers control hair ends & prevent fishhooks during perm wrapping.

Q81.

Answer: A

Explanation: Disulfide bonds, strong chemical bonds, contribute significantly to hair strength.

Q82.

Answer: D

Explanation: Fine hair processes color faster due to tightly grouped melanin granules.

Q83.

Answer: C

Explanation: Cotton is placed to prevent the lightener from contacting the scalp during the application.

Q84.

Answer: C

Explanation: Chemical hair relaxing transforms curly hair into a straighter or smoother form.

Q85.

Answer: B

Explanation: Hydroxide neutralization deactivates alkaline residues left in the hair by the relaxer.

Q86.

Answer: A

Explanation: Low-pH waves are weak and not widely used.

Q87.

Answer: C

Explanation: Protects the cosmetologist from chemical exposure.

Q88.

Answer: C

Explanation: Straight hair is often sleek, shiny, and easy to manage.

Q89.

Answer: B

Explanation: It is essential to use a special cleanser for eye because it helps in preventing eye damage, ensuring a comfortable and safe facial treatment experiences.

Q90.

Answer: C

Explanation: In this case, medium pores, good circulation, and tends toward dryness are the characteristics of combination/normal while oily in the T-zone.

Q91.

Answer: B

Explanation: Even with precautions, there is still a chance of contamination, presenting risk to both other clients and the cosmetologists.

Q92.

Answer: C

Explanation: In the context of effective facial hair removal, An Electric Facial Epilator reduces pain by pulling out hair from the root, offering a convenient DIY option.

Q93.

Answer: B

Explanation: Please note that enhanced circulation during facial steaming increases oxygen supply to the skin, promoting a healthier complexion.

Q94.

Answer: A

Explanation: Petroleum jelly which is a cost-effective emollient, effectively moisturizes dry, aging skin, minimizing moisture loss and providing long-lasting hydration.

Q95.

Answer: B

Explanation: Including safe handling procedures, MSDS provides important information, ensuring salon professional can take necessary precautions and are aware of possible hazards.

Q96.

Answer: D

Explanation: Please note that the cosmetologists should ask about a client's medication because it helps to identify contraindications for facial treatments, ensuring effective and safe skincare.

Q97.

Answer: A

Explanation: Primary purpose of applying a moist, warm towel is softening the area, facilitating a comfortable and effective shaving.

Q98.

Answer: C

Explanation: In makeup application, the main purpose of contouring and highlighting is to hide imperfections and accentuate good features, ensuring an enhanced and balanced appearance.

Q99.

Answer: B

Explanation: Please note that high-frequency current has a germicidal effect that makes it suitable for acne-prone skin by promoting clear complexion and reducing bacteria.

Q100.

Answer: B

Explanation: In the context of comprehensive nail care analysis, understanding nail conditions is essential to ensure safe and appropriate services.

Q101.

Answer: B

Explanation: Brittle nail syndrome might restrict but not entirely prevent a service, while nail separation or severe psoriasis could prevent services.

Q102.

Answer: C

Explanation: In the context of long-lasting manicure for upcoming vacation, gel nail polish offers durability and extended wear.

Q103.

Answer: A

Explanation: For client with nail ridges, nail buffer is the most suitable product that provides a polished and smoother surface on the natural nail.

Q104.

Answer: C

Explanation: Before performing nail services, it is essential for cosmetologists to record a client's medical history to identify potential risks or contraindications.

Q105.

Answer. B

Explanation: During paraffin treatments to relax the skin and enhance lotion absorption involve dipping hands in melted paraffin.

Q106.

Answer. C

Explanation: Please note that, as per EPA requirements total immersion of implements ensure proper disinfection, meeting the regulatory standards for maintaining a hygienic salon environment.

Q107.

Answer. A

Explanation: Implement should be properly cleaned and disinfected after each use, taking approximately 20 minutes, if there's only one set.

Q108.

Answer. B

Explanation: As stated in the options, ignoring ergonomic challenges in the nail care industry may lead to decreased client satisfaction.

Q109.

Answer. C

Explanation: To prevent lifting and cracking in acrylic nail enhancements, maintain regular maintenance, which reducing the risk of infections and other problems.

Q110.

Answer: C

Explanation: For reshaping and durability the apex is removed, and the entire acrylic nail is thinned down in rebalancing.

Cosmetology Exam Practice Test-2

Q1. In cosmetology practice, what are the important microorganisms to control among the following?

(A) Algae and protozoa

(B) Bacteria, fungus, and virus

(C) Insects and mites

(D) Mold and mildew

Q2. Identify the type of virus from the options given below which can cause hepatitis. Why it is more easily contracted than HIV?

(A) Hepatitis B; resistant to disinfectants

(B) Hepatitis C; long survival on surfaces

(C) Hepatitis A; present in body fluids

(D) Hepatitis D; rapid transmission through air

Q3. To disinfect foot spa after each client. What is the recommended method to ensure complete sanitation?

(A) Wiping with a towel

(B) Circulating a disinfectant solution

(C) Using a chelating detergent

(D) Applying an antiseptic spray

Q4. In cosmetology, while handling phenolic disinfectants. What preventive measure should be taken?

(A) Apply directly to the skin

(B) Mix without gloves

(C) Avoid skin contact

(D) Dispose in regular trash

Q5. While handling disinfectants in cosmetology. Which safety measure is necessary?

(A) Wear gloves and safety glasses

(B) Apply disinfectant directly to the skin

(C) Mix water into the disinfectant

(D) Store disinfectants within reach of children

Q6. After utilization of single use objects present in the client packs. Which method should be used according to cosmetology protocols?

(A) Dispose of them immediately

(B) Reuse without cleaning

(C) Clean, disinfect, and store for reuse

(D) Store in an airtight container

Q7. To avoid cross contamination, while handling salon equipment. Which step is essential?

(A) Storing tools in a closed, damp environment

(B) Sterilizing tools at the end of the day

(C) Regularly cleaning and sanitizing tools

(D) Using tools without inspection

Q8. In the salon, to prevent cross contamination among clients. How is the utilization of single use items helpful?

(A) By promoting tool sharing

(B) By encouraging tool storage without inspection

(C) By eliminating the need for cleaning

(D) By minimizing the risk of transferring microorganisms

Q9. For not having MSDSs for harmful products in the salon. What consequence may a salon face, in accordance with federal regulation?

(A) License renewal

(B) Client complaints

(C) Fines

(D) Marketing opportunities

Q10. According to EPA, which factor EPA consider to categorize disinfectants utilized in salon?

(A) Based on scent

(B) Based on color

(C) Based on safety

(D) Based on type (e.g., hospital or tuberculocidal)

Q11. How does the EPA's licensing of disinfectants impact cosmetologists' choices in salon products?

(A) By limiting product availability

(B) By ensuring product safety

(C) By encouraging excessive product use

(D) By promoting trendy salon designs

Q12. If gloves come into contact with blood. Which step must be taken before removing gloves, in accordance with OSHA protocols?

(A) Wash hands thoroughly

(B) Disinfect gloves

(C) Clean workstation

(D) Immersing tools in bleach solution

Q13. In case of an exposure incident, a practitioner needs to clean tools, which come into contact with blood or body fluids. What should a practitioner used for this purpose?

(A) Soap and water

(B) Alcohol-based cleaner

(C) Bleach solution for 5 minutes

(D) EPA-registered disinfectant for 10 minutes

Q14. In cosmetology practices, to maintain optimal hygiene and safety. What is the recommended frequency for changing disinfectants?

(A) Weekly

(B) Monthly

(C) Every day, or more if soiled

(D) Annually

Q15. What is the primary function of sebum, which is produced by sebaceous glands?

(A) Hair cleansing

(B) Blood circulation

(C) Scalp moisturization

(D) Thermal regulation

Q16. From the given layers, which layer of the epidermis is made up of cells that are almost dead and pushed to the skin's surface?

(A) Stratum lucidum

(B) Stratum granulosum

(C) Basal cell layer

(D) Spiny layer

Q17. Which skin layer from the following forms the nail grooves, and ensures the nail moves as it grows?

(A) Eponychium

(B) Hyponychium

(C) Nail fold

(D) Cuticle

Q18. Due to bacterial infection, which condition from the following involves the inflammation of hair follicles?

(A) Folliculitis

(B) Seborrheic dermatitis

(C) Tinea capitis

(D) Telogen effluvium

Q19. Due to excessive pulling from tight hairstyles, what scalp condition causes hair loss?

(A) Trichotillomania

(B) Folliculitis

(C) Traction alopecia

(D) Seborrheic dermatitis

Q20. Which of the following skin layer composes of blood vessels, nerves, glands, collagen, and elastin?

(A) Epidermis

(B) Subcutis

(C) Dermis

(D) Basal cell layer

Q21. Which of the following characterizes, forming a black band within the nail plate darkening the fingernails or toenails?

(A) Onychocryptosis

(B) Plicatured nail

(C) Melanonychia

(D) Onycholysis

Q22. Among the following nerves, which nerve affects the skin of the lower lip and chin?

(A) Infraorbital nerve

(B) Mental nerve

(C) Nasal nerve

(D) Zygomatic nerve

Q23. The nerve affecting the skin on the outer side and back of the foot and leg is the:

(A) Sural nerve

(B) Tibial nerve

(C) Dorsal nerve

(D) Peroneal nerve

Q24. From below below-mentioned nerves, which nerve mainly affects the sensation of the forehead and the scalp up to the top of the head?

(A) Infraorbital nerve

(B) Supratrochlear nerve

(C) Supraorbital nerve

(D) Nasal nerve

Q25. What role does the circulatory system play in the application of makeup?

(A) Determines hair growth patterns

(B) Influences skin hydration levels

(C) Regulates nail polish adhesion

(D) Provides nutrients to the scalp

Q26. In what manner, does understanding of blood circulation impact hair-related methods used by cosmetology professionals?

(A) Predicts nail growth patterns

(B) Influences hair follicle health

(C) Minimizes skin dryness

(D) Determines appropriate makeup application techniques

Q27. From the given options, which bone supports the tongue and its muscles?

(A) Hyoid bone

(B) Cervical vertebrae

(C) Sternum

(D) Scapula

Q28. Which bone helps in maintaining the foot's stability and movement and also supports the lateral side?

(A) Navicular

(B) Cuboid

(C) Cuneiform

(D) Calcaneus

Q29. From the given options, which ion affects the pH of salon products and is responsible for acidity in water?

(A) Anion

(B) Cation

(C) Hydroxide ion

(D) Hydrogen ion

Q30. Considering the following options, which aspect defines a pure substance and gives it unique properties?

(A) Physical combination

(B) Variable proportions

(C) Chemical combination

(D) Physical mixture

Q31. What is difference between a physical change and a chemical change?

(A) Physical changes involve a new substance.

(B) Chemical changes alter physical properties.

(C) Physical changes result from chemical reactions.

(D) Chemical changes create new substances.

Q32. During the rapid oxidation of a chemical substance such as combustion of a match, which of the following reaction is responsible for creating heat and light?

(A) Neutralization

(B) Oxidation

(C) Reduction

(D) Polymerization

Q33. Which of the following element's absence characterizes inorganic substances?

(A) Hydrogen

(B) Oxygen

(C) Carbon

(D) Nitrogen

Q34. In the field of chemistry, a substance having a pH under 7.0 indicates:

(A) Alkaline

(B) Neutral

(C) Acidic

(D) Exothermic

Q35. Based on changing in pH levels, how do amphoteric surfactants respond?

(A) Maintain a constant charge

(B) Change from positive to negative

(C) Exhibit no surfactant properties

(D) Remain zwitterionic

Q36. When testing the pH of non-aqueous products, why utilization of distilled water recommended?

(A) To enhance fragrance

(B) To ensure accurate pH readings

(C) To improve texture

(D) To add minerals

Q37. In cosmetic products, what is the role of surfactants?

(A) Provide color

(B) Enhance fragrance

(C) Lower water surface tension

(D) Extend shelf life

Q38. Due to cleaning and lathering properties, which of the following surfactants is utilized in personal care products?

(A) Titanium Dioxide

(B) Sodium Lauryl Sulfate (SLS)

(C) Citric Acid

(D) Toluene

Q39. Which part of the skin is responsible for shafts that keep the hair soft? Please select only one option.

(A) Papilla

(B) Epidermis

(C) Dermis

(D) Hair follicle

Q40. During a consultation for the cosmetologist in a salon. What type of questions is crucial to understand the clients need?

(A) Personal questions

(B) Generic questions

(C) Stylist preferences

(D) Client-focused questions

Q41. It is important for cosmetologists to talk with clients about their health. Why?

(A) Maintains confidentiality

(B) Demonstrates professionalism

(C) Validates product choices

(D) Enhances artistic skills

Q42. To prevent PFB, how does a shaver or razor with an elevated blade contribute?

(A) Cutting hair too short

(B) Creating a low-oxygen environment

(C) Shaving against hair growth

(D) Acting as a bumper to stop hair from being cut too short

Q43. In what condition does a therapist proceed with treatment, subject to a doctor's note and modification of techniques?

(A) Immediate contraindication

(B) Total contraindication

(C) General contraindication

(D) Relative contraindication

Q44. During beauty treatments, which condition could initiate the spread of infection including, skin-to-skin contact?

(A) Allergies

(B) Conjunctivitis

(C) Bruising

(D) Swelling

Q45. During the hair color formulation process, from which area might color data be needed?

(A) Temples

(B) Hairline

(C) Occipital line

(D) Crown of the head

Q46. The sudden onset with nonscarring, what is the primary cause of noninflammatory alopecia?

(A) Tinea capitis

(B) Trichotillomania

(C) Telogen effluvium

(D) Androgenetic alopecia

Q47. To treat female pattern hair loss, in addition to topical minoxidil what medical therapy is successfully used?

(A) Finasteride

(B) Spironolactone

(C) Dutasteride

(D) Oral contraceptives

Q48. For anti-inflammatory effects what type of medication is used and treatment options for lichen planopilaris?

(A) Finasteride

(B) Doxycycline

(C) Hydroxychloroquine

(D) Minoxidil

Q49. To relieve dandruff due to its anti-inflammatory and anti-microbial properties, what can be an effective quick fix?

(A) Olive Oil

(B) Coconut Water

(C) Apple Cider Vinegar

(D) Argan Oil

Q50. For each individual appointment, what is an essential element to include in the client record card?

(A) Date of birth

(B) Treatment name

(C) Emergency contact

(D) Treatment results

Q51. To ensure clients are serviced with properly cleaned and disinfected tools each day, which of the following is crucial step in cosmetology?

(A) Salon ambiance

(B) Sufficient supply of disinfected tools

(C) Variety of brushes

(D) Decorative barrettes

Q52. For isolating hair sections during cutting, coloring, or styling, which of the following tools is essential in cosmetology?

(A) Hair clipper

(B) Hair roller

(C) Hairpin

(D) Hair brush

Q53. In cosmetology training, what is the primary purpose of using mannequin heads?

(A) Decorative styling

(B) Client use

(C) Practice new techniques

(D) Maintain cleanliness

Q54. Why should cosmetologists use only cleaned, disinfected, and properly stored tools on clients?

(A) To enhance stylist comfort

(B) To minimize salon costs

(C) To ensure client satisfaction

(D) To save time during services

Q55. Which of the following tools do cosmetologists use to create crimps in the hair, providing a textured and voluminous appearance?

A) Hair roller

B) Crimping iron

C) Hairbrush

D) Hairpin

Q56. In cosmetology, how do electric clippers contribute to achieving specific hair lengths?

A) Adds shine to the hair

B) Achieves closer cuts

C) Creates textured styles

D) Precision cutting

Q57. What is the reason behind using mannequin heads with diverse hair textures for practice?

A) For decorative purposes

(B) To promote hair health

(C) To practice various techniques

(D) To add volume

Q58. In cosmetology setting, how does a thermal brush differ from other brushes?

(A) Adds volume

(B) Detangles hair

(C) Requires heat for styling

(D) Enhances shine

Q59. In cosmetology settings, why it is crucial to store clean and disinfected towels in closed containers labeled "clean"?

A) Adds comfort to the client

B) Ensures hygiene and safety

C) Enhances hair color absorption

D) Creates volume in hairstyles

Q60. For creating a layered hair cut rather than a blunt one, which of the following type of shears is ideal?

(A) Short shears

(B) Long shears

(C) Thinning/blending shears

(D) Texturizing shears

Q61. In cosmetology, what is the main objective of using a steam diffuser?

(A) Adding volume

(B) Creating curls

(C) Straightening the hair

(D) Moisturizing and conditioning the hair

Q62. During cosmetology services, why it is recommended to use only one plug in each outlet?

(A) Enhances creativity

(B) Adds moisture to the hair

(C) Prevents circuit overload

(D) Improves hair shine

Q63. Different from other treatments, what purpose does a leave in conditioner serve in hair care practices?

(A) Rinsed out after detangling

(B) Applied before shampooing

(C) Applied to hair and not rinsed out

(D) Used only during chemical services

Q64. When should the application of dry shampoo be approached with caution in cosmetology practices?

(A) Before chemical service

(B) After applying conditioner

(C) During scalp massage

(D) After a clarifying shampoo

Q65. Distinguishing it from other interventions, what role does high frequency treatment play in scalp procedures?

A) Hair coloring

B) Relaxation

C) Stimulation or soothing

D) Straightening

Q66. What can additional salon treatments and home care products help address in an antidandruff treatment?

A) Increase oiliness

B) Restore moisture

C) Promote tingling effect

D) Stimulate microcirculation

Q67. Which draping type is appropriately used for optimal functionality in the context of shampoo and styling service?

(A) Cutting or styling draping

(B) Chemical service draping

(C) Dry shampoo draping

(D) Shampoo draping

Q68. On which occasions is the utilization of cutting or styling draping most appropriate in cosmetology procedures?

(A) Before any service

(B) After shampooing

(C) During chemical services or treatments

(D) Throughout the entire service

Q69. What sets apart hair type from hair texture, providing clarity on their definition cosmetology distinctions?

(A) Hair type reflects shine

(B) Hair texture refers to single strands

(C) Hair type is about how hair feels

(D) Hair texture describes the head of hair

Q70. Which layer unifies all types of hair textures universally among the components of hair structure?

(A) Cortex

(B) Cuticle

(C) Medulla

(D) None of the above

Q71. For hair styles suitable for clients, in the context how does a hairstylist develop a visual understanding?

(A) By reading books

(B) Only through book learning

(C) Through experience and trial-and-error

(D) By avoiding new techniques

Q72. To create harmony in hair styles, which design principle is important?

(A) Harmony

(B) Balance

(C) Rhythm

(D) Emphasis

Q73. For hair extensions, what is the recommended distance from the hairline?

A) 1 inch

B) 2 inches

C) 0.5 inch

D) 3 inches

Q74. In the context of hair cutting, what is the main purpose of a clipper?

(A) Remove bulk

(B) Create blunt lines

(C) Section hair

(D) Shave hair to the scalp

Q75. Why is finished styling often considered important to a customer's decision in the context of hair styling?

(A) It's a subjective preference

(B) It showcases the cut or color

(C) It reflects the stylist's personality

(D) Clients typically ignore the finished style

Q76. In the content of hair styling, what is the main purpose of a thermal iron?

(A) Detangling

(B) Straightening

(C) Wet setting

(D) Coloring

Q77. Why is client consultation important in the context of wig services?

(A) Enhancing stylist creativity

(B) Offering protection for both client and stylist

(C) Demonstrating fashion trends

(D) Reducing salon costs

Q78. For the integration hairpiece, which type of client is not recommended?

A) Those with total hair loss

B) Those with thick hair

C) Those with thinning hair

D) Those with curly hair

Q79. In the context of certification training, what method of hair extension attachment is required?

(A) Linking method

(B) Fusion method

(C) Tube method

(D) Bonding method

Q80. What does reduction entail in the context of the chemistry of permanent waving?

(A) Addition of oxygen

(B) Removal of hydrogen

(C) Addition of sulfur

(D) Removal of ammonia

Q81. In the hair, what role do salt bonds play in the hair?

A) Provide color

B) Add shine

C) Contribute to strength

D) Easily broken by changes in pH

Q82. Why is it essential to grasp the concept of hair density when applying hair color?

A) Influences color vibrancy

B) Ensures proper coverage

C) Affects shine

D) Minimizes frizz

Q83. In highlighting, what technique involves pulling strands through a perforated cap?

(A) Foil technique

(B) Baliage technique

(C) Cap technique

(D) Free-form technique

Q84. In hydroxide relaxers, which ingredient exhibits a very high pH and is responsible for breaking disulfide bonds?

(A) ATG

(B) Hydrogen peroxide

(C) Lanthionine

(D) Ion hydroxide

Q85. In Keratin Straightening Treatments, what is the primary element that requires specific ventilation for safety?

(A) Silicone polymers

(B) Keratin

(C) Formaldehyde

(D) Preconditioner

Q86. In permanent waving, what is entailed in the technique of "on-base placement"?

(A) Wrapping at 45 degrees below the base

(B) Placing rod perpendicular to base

(C) Wrapping at a 90-degree angle

(D) Wrapping beyond perpendicular to the base

Q87. During a perm application, what should be done with wet cotton or towels during a perm application?

(A) Save them for later use

(B) Reapply them after drying

(C) Dispose of them immediately

(D) Use them on other clients

Q88. What kind of Hair is characterized by tight or loose curls, coils, or spirals and may require specialized care?

(A) Straight hair

(B) Wavy hair

(C) Curly hair

(D) Coily/Kinky hair

Q89. During a facial consultation with a client, what should be the primary focus?

(A) Selling retail products

(B) Recommending salon treatments

(C) Understanding client's needs

(D) Discussing the salon's quiet area

Q90. Considering the following option, which skin type has overactive sebaceous glands, and is prone to blackheads and blemishes?

(A) Oily skin

(B) Dry skin

(C) Combination/normal skin

(D) Sensitive skin

Q91. In the context of beauty therapy, what is the recommended actions for recently consumed alcohol or drugs?

(A) Proceed with caution

(B) Refuse treatment

(C) Consult a physician

(D) Offer alternative treatments

Q92. Which of the following is a key benefit of utilizing Facial Cleansing Brush?

(A) Increasing facial hair growth

(B) Reducing wrinkles

(C) Adding shine to nails

(D) Boosting circulation

Q93. Which of the following role does facial steaming enhance for better product absorption?

(A) Hair growth

(B) Blood clotting

(C) Pore closure

(D) Product penetration

Q94. From the given options, what is the known characterization of alpha hydroxy acids (AHAs) and beta hydroxy acids (BHAs) in skincare practices?

(A) Hair coloration

(B) Exfoliating skin

(C) Nail strengthening

(D) Sun protection

Q95. In the view of renewing collagen and changing cell growth, which chemicals are considered superior to many masks, scrubs, and tonners?

(A) Salicylic acid

(B) Alpha hydroxy acids (AHAs)

(C) Retinol

(D) Hyaluronic acid

Q96. From the following options, which message movement is used to stimulate muscle and impact a healthy grow?

(A) Petrissage

(B) Effleurage

(C) Tapotement

(D) Friction

Q97. In order to destroy hair growth cells, which permanent hair removal method uses a fine needle-shaped electrode and an electric current?

(A) Photoepilation

(B) Laser hair removal

(C) Electrolysis

(D) Depilatories

Q98. From the following options, what approach is advisable for cosmetologists to take in makeup application for clients?

(A) Applying uniform looks

(B) Focusing on facial flaws

(C) Considering individual needs

(D) Prioritizing bold colors

Q99. Considering the following option, what is the main function of light-emitting diode (LED) treatment?

(A) Warming tissues

(B) Minimizing redness

(C) Softening and emulsifying sebum

(D) Enhancing natural skin tone

Q100. Considering the following options what is the primary purpose of salon intake form?

(A) Record client allergies

(B) Assess service quality

(C) Evaluate salon staff

(D) Expedite payment processing

Q101. During a client consultation in nail services, what is the main purpose of recording responses and observations?

(A) Monitoring hair growth patterns

(B) Understanding skin pigmentation

(C) Customizing nail art designs

(D) Noting any nail disorders or habits

Q102. Which of the following conditions might restrict but not necessarily prevent a nail service?

(A) Beau's lines

(B) Leuconychia

(C) Longitudinal melanonychia

(D) Onychomadesis

Q103. Considering the options, which of the following product or service would be recommended to the client by a cosmetologist for long-lasting nail color without chipping?

(A) Regular nail polish

(B) Shellac or gel polish

(C) Acrylic dipping powder

(D) French manicure treatment

Q104. In a salon record-keeping process why it is essential to maintain client record card?

(A) To track salon marketing strategies

(B) To monitor employee attendance

(C) To record client preferences and service history

(D) To analyze salon revenue

Q105. In a manicure what is the primary purpose of a nail buffer?

(A) Filing nails

(B) Shaping nails

(C) Adding shine and smoothing ridges

(D) Removing nail polish

Q106. During a manicure, how should a wooden pusher be held for effective use?

(A) Like a spoon

(B) Like a fork

(C) Like a brush

(D) Like a pencil

Q107. From the following options, if the disinfectant solution appears cloudy, what should be done?

(A) Replace the solution

(B) Stir the solution

(C) Add more disinfectant

(D) Continue using the solution

Q108. In cosmetology, who could benefit the most from the suggested shoe according to the options?

(A) Salon owners

(B) Clients

(C) Stylists

(D) Medical professionals

Q109. What is the purpose to applying a pink, sheer white, or peach color polish in the French and American manicures?

(A) Adds drama

(B) Enhances shine

(C) Provides a natural appearance

(D) Covers imperfections

Q110. In the process of maintenance, what is the purpose of smoothing the ledge between new growth and acrylic nail?

(A) Enhance color consistency

(B) Prevent discoloration

(C) Avoid damage to natural nail

(D) Add shine to the free edge

Test 2 Answer Key

Q1.

Answer: B

Explanation: For infection prevention in cosmetology practices, the three categories of microorganisms such as viruses, fungi and bacteria are crucial to control.

Q2.

Answer: B

Explanation: Hepatitis C emphasizing the need for thorough cleaning. It is essential to note, it can survive on surfaces for extended periods of time.

Q3.

Answer: B

Explanation: In context of above question, it is essential to disinfect foot spas after each client for hygiene. To ensure thorough disinfection, circulate the solution to reach all areas.

Q4.

Answer: C

Explanation: Please note that, phenolic disinfectants needs caution to handle. Because in cosmetology practices, it is necessary to avoid skin contact with them.

Q5.

Answer: A

Explanation: The eye and skin damage can be prevented, while handling disinfectants. For this purpose wearing gloves and safety glasses is essential.

Q6.

Answer: A

Explanation: To prevent contamination which can spread through single use items. Please note that dispose them instantly after use.

Q7.

Answer: C

Explanation: In salon, spread of microorganisms can be prevented by regular cleaning and sanitation of tools. Additionally, these preventive measures can also reduce the danger of cross contamination.

Q8.

Answer: D

Explanation: In cosmetology practices, the danger of microorganisms transfer is reduced remarkably due to single use items. Please note that it can also prevent the cross-contamination.

Q9.

Answer: C

Explanation: The availability of MSDSs emphasize the significance of compliance with federal regulations to ensure salon safety. Please note, for not having MSDSs can result in fines to the practitioners.

Q10.

Answer: D

Explanation: Please note that, EPA categorize disinfectant based on types such as hospital or tuberculocidal. In salon settings, EPA also specifies their applications.

Q11.

Answer: B

Explanation: Please note that, EPA licensing ensures the safety of disinfectants. To ensure safety, guide cosmetologists to choose products that meet safety standards.

Q12.

Answer: A

Explanation: Keeping in view the OSHA protocols, if blood comes into contact with gloves. It is essential to wash hands before removing gloves.

Q13.

Answer: D

Explanation: In accordance with EPA guidelines, to ensure complete sterilization in case of an exposure incident. It is recommended to disinfect properly with EPA registered solution for 10 minutes.

Q14.

Answer: C

Explanation: During cosmetology practices, if the solution becomes soiled or contaminated. Consequently, to maintain hygiene, disinfectants should be changed daily, or more often.

Q15.

Answer: C

Explanation: The primary function of sebum, which is produced by sebaceous glands is to moisturize the scalp and hair. It prevents excessive dryness by providing essential moisture and conditioning effects.

Q16.

Answer: B

Explanation: Stratum granulosum is the layer of epidermis, in which the cells are nearly dead and pushed upward to the replace the skin surface layer.

Q17.

Answer: C

Explanation: Nail folds form the nail grooves, which surround the nail plate, and make sure that the nail moves as it grows.

Q18.

Answer: A

Explanation: Folliculitis is caused by bacterial infection that leads to inflamed hair follicles.

Q19.

Answer: C

Explanation: Traction alopecia is the condition, which leads to hair loss from excessive pulling caused by tight hairstyles.

Q20.

Answer: C

Explanation: The dermis is the skin layer, which contains blood vessels, nerves, and essential proteins like: collagen and elastin.

Q21.

Answer: C

Explanation: Melanonychia presents as darkening of nails, which forms black bands within the nail plate.

Q22.

Answer: B

Explanation: The mental nerve affects the skin of the lower lip and chin, influencing sensation and movement in that area.

Q23.

Answer: A

Explanation: The sural nerve delivers impulses to the outer side and back of the foot and leg, contributing to sensory functions in that region.

Q24.

Answer: C

Explanation: The supraorbital nerve mainly supplies sensation to the forehead and scalp up to the top of the head.

Q25.

Answer: B

Explanation: The Circulatory system maintains skin hydration levels, which helps a great deal in the application and appearance of makeup on the skin.

Q26.

Answer: B

Explanation: Understanding blood circulation has a great impact on hair-related methods used by cosmetology professionals. It can influence hair follicle health.

Q27.

Answer: A

Explanation: The hyoid bone provides support for the tongue and its associated muscles, which helps in speech and swallowing.

Q28.

Answer: B

Explanation: The cuboid bone supports the lateral side of the foot. It offers stability and facilitates movement in the foot's structure.

Q29.

Answer: D

Explanation: In the context of acidity in water, hydrogen ion is acidic and affects the pH of salon products.

Q30.

Answer: C

Explanation: Chemical combination with definite proportions defines a pure substance. Unlike physical mixtures, it exhibits its unique properties.

Q31.

Answer: D

Explanation: Please note that chemical change results in the creation of new substances, while physical change alter physical properties or form.

Q32.

Answer: B

Explanation: In salon services, oxidation reactions are fundamental to chemical changes. These reactions produce heat and light.

Q33.

Answer: C

Explanation: Organic substances contain carbon atoms in their molecular structure while inorganic substances lack carbon.

Q34.

Answer: C

Explanation: A substance having a pH under 7.0 indicates acidic in nature while substances with pH above 7.0 are alkaline or basic in nature.

Q35.

Answer: B

Explanation: Due to changing in pH levels, please note that amphoteric surfactants change their charge from positive to negative.

Q36.

Answer: B

Explanation: To ensure accurate pH readings, utilization of distilled water is recommended. It provides a neutral base for testing non-aqueous products.

Q37.

Answer: C

Explanation: In cosmetic products, the role of surfactants is to lower water surface tension. It helps in product lathering and enables soap to mix with water.

Q38.

Answer: B

Explanation: In the context of personal care products, Sodium Lauryl Sulfate is a surfactant that helps in cleaning and lathering and lowers water surface tension.

Q39.

Answer: B

Explanation: The epidermis layer is responsible for specialized cells that produce shafts contributing to the soft texture of the hair.

Q40.

Answer: D

Explanation: During a consultation, client focused questions are essential for understanding the client's needs and preferences.

Q41.

Answer: B

Explanation: Discussing a client's health is crucial for building solid client cosmetologist relationships. It establishes trust and demonstrates professionalism.

Q42.

Answer: D

Explanation: During shaving, the elevated blade acts as a bumper by preventing the hair from being cut too short.

Q43.

Answer: D

Explanation: The condition is a relative contraindication, permitting treatment with doctor approval and requiring adjustments to techniques based on the severity of the client's condition.

Q44.

Answer: B

Explanation: During beauty treatments, conjunctivitis poses infection spread risks, especially those including skin-to-skin contact around the face.

Q45.

Answer: D

Explanation: During the strand testing, color information from the crown of the head may be necessary for complete the formulation process.

Q46.

Answer: C

Explanation: Nonscarring, noninflammatory alopecia with a sudden onset" is clear, but you may consider rephrasing for conciseness, such as "Alopecia with a sudden onset.

Q47.

Answer: B

Explanation: In addition to topical minoxidil, spironolactone medication is successfully used in treating female pattern hair loss.

Q48.

Answer: B

Explanation: Doxycycline, known for its anti-inflammatory effects, is a treatment option for lichen planopilaris.

Q49.

Answer: C

Explanation: Apple cider vinegar, known for its anti-inflammatory and anti-microbial properties, serves as a quick fix to relieve dandruff.

Q50.

Answer: B

Explanation: Including the name of the treatment performed, specifying products used, and detailing the treatment protocol is essential for each appointment record.

Q51.

Answer: B

Explanation: To meet hygiene standards for each client in cosmetology, a sufficient supply of disinfected tools is necessary.

Q52.

Answer: C

Explanation: In cosmetology, hairpins are necessary for isolating and securing hair sections during cutting, coloring, or styling.

Q53.

Answer: C

Explanation: Mannequin heads are used in cosmetology to practice new hair techniques.

Q54.

Answer: C

Explanation: It is recommended to use only cleaned, disinfected, and properly stored tools during services to ensure client satisfaction, hygiene, and professionalism.

Q55.

Answer: B

Explanation: In cosmetology, crimping irons are used to create crimps in the hair, adding texture and volume to the hair.

Q56.

Answer: B

Explanation: Cosmetologists use electric clippers to achieve closer cuts, particularly in styles that require specific hair lengths.

Q57.

Answer: C

Explanation: To practice different techniques on various hair types, mannequin heads with diverse textures are used in cosmetology.

Q58.

Answer: C

Explanation: Cosmetologists use thermal brushes to achieve specific hairstyles. A thermal brush requires heat for styling, making it suitable for use with blow dryers.

Q59.

Answer: B

Explanation: Cosmetologists store clean and disinfected towels in closed containers labeled "clean" to promote hygiene and safety.

Q60.

Answer: C

Explanation: Cosmetologists use thinning/blending shears to create a layered cut that enhances the texture of the hair, providing distinct results compared to blunt cuts achieved with regular shears.

Q61.

Answer: D

Explanation: Steam diffusers contribute in providing hydration and improving overall hair health. Cosmetologists use steam diffusers to moisturize and condition the hair.

Q62.

Answer: C

Explanation: For ensuring safety and effective electrical usage, only one plug should be used in each outlet to prevent circuit overload.

Q63.

Answer: C

Explanation: Offering prolonged nourishment and protection, leave in conditioners play a unique role as they are applied to the hair and left without rinsing.

Q64.

Answer: A

Explanation: To mitigate the risk of potential damage to the hair exercise caution with dry shampoo before a chemical service.

Q65.

Answer: C

Explanation: Enhancing the overall procedural experience, high frequency treatments are specifically employed to stimulate or soothe the scalp.

Q66.

Answer: B

Explanation: During an antidandruff treatment additional salon treatments and home care products helps to restore moisture.

Q67.

Answer: D

Explanation: Ensuring practicality and client comfort, shampoo draping is specifically designed for shampoo and styling services.

Q68.

Answer: C

Explanation: During chemical services or treatments for targeted protection and efficiency, cutting or styling draping is specifically implemented.

Q69.

Answer: B

Explanation: Hair texture specifically examines the unique attributes of each strand, while hair type encompasses the entire head.

Q70.

Answer: B

Explanation: Contributing to overall hair structure, the cuticle layer serves as a common element across all hair textures.

Q71.

Answer: C

Explanation: In this context for different clients. Experimentation and trial and error help the hairstylist identify the best design decisions.

Q72.

Answer: B

Explanation: In the context of hairstyling for a pleasant hairstyle. Whether for a symmetrical or asymmetrical look, balance is important.

Q73.

Answer: A

Explanation: For attaching hair extensions the recommended distance from the hairline is 1 inch. As a general rule, stay 1 inch away from the hairline when growing hair.

Q74.

Answer: D

Explanation: Clippers provide accuracy in various styles. They are mainly used for short haircuts. They can also shave hair to the scalp.

Q75.

Answer: B

Explanation: In hair styling. Clients often judge hairstylist work based on the finished look, regardless of cut or color.

Q76.

Answer: B

Explanation: In this context, thermal irons alter hydrogen bonds to produce a straight conformation. And they use heat to change the texture of the hair.

Q77.

Answer: B

Explanation: Client consultation is important for wig services. They ensure realistic expectations and prevent disappointment. And protects both the client and the stylist.

Q78.

Answer: A

Explanation: In this context. Integration hairpieces are not recommended for clients with complete hair loss.

Q79.

Answer: B

Explanation: In certification training for proper application and removal. Hair extensions require a fusion procedure.

Q80.

Answer: B

Explanation: Reduction in permanent waving involves adding hydrogen to break disulfide bonds.

Q81.

Answer: D

Explanation: Salt bonds are easily broken by pH changes, influencing hair strength.

Q82.

Answer: B

Explanation: Proper consideration of hair density is crucial for achieving even color coverage.

Q83.

Answer: C

Explanation: Cap technique involves using a cap to pull strands through for highlighting.

Q84.

Answer: D

Explanation: Ion hydroxide in hydroxide relaxers, with a high pH, breaks disulfide bonds.

Q85.

Answer: C

Explanation: Keratin treatments release formaldehyde when heated, requiring specific ventilation.

Q86.

Answer: D

Explanation: On-base placement is beyond 90 degrees, providing volume.

Q87.

Answer: C

Explanation: Prevents potential chemical reactions and ensures safety.

Q88.

Answer: C

Explanation: Curly hair forms tight or loose curls, coils or spirals and may be prone to frizz requiring specialized care.

Q89.

Answer: C

Explanation: Understanding the client's needs with the help of effective questioning is the primary focus of a facial consultation.

Q90.

Answer: A

Explanation: Overactive sebaceous glands define oily skin, leading to blemishes, a greasy shine, and blackheads.

Q91.

Answer: B

Explanation: Please note that the treatment should be refused in the above situation, because drugs and alcohols can impact blood pressure and consent, making beauty therapy unsafe.

Q92.

Answer: D

Explanation: Key benefit of utilizing a Facial Cleansing Brush is promoting blood flow, contributing to youthful and healthy skin by minimizing the appearance of pores and boosting circulation.

Q93.

Answer: D

Explanation: Skin preparation through facial steaming enhances absorption of serums, toners and moisturizers, leading to enhanced product effectiveness.

Q94.

Answer: B

Explanation: Please note that the known characterization of AHAs and BHAs are that they are chemical exfoliants renowned for improving skin texture by removing dead cells, promoting a revitalized and smoother complexion.

Q95.

Answer: B

Explanation: Alpha hydroxy acids are chemical exfoliants that excel in promoting collagen renewal and changing cell growth, surpassing many other skincare products.

Q96.

Answer: C

Explanation: Please note that tapotement movements enhance skin health and stimulate muscles, providing a revitalizing effect during facial massage.

Q97.

Answer: C

Explanation: In order to destroy hair growth cells, Electrolysis is a permanent hair removal method, using a needle and electric current.

Q98.

Answer: C

Explanation: Please note that in order to achieve a personalized and satisfying result, makeup application must consider individual client needs and preferences.

Q99.

Answer: B

Explanation: Light-emitting diode (LED) treatment is responsible to minimizes redness, improve skin texture, and warms lower-level tissues, making it suitable for acne-prone skin and cosmetic applications.

Q100.

Answer: A

Explanation: Please note that the primary purpose of salon intake forms is to record client allergies for personalized service.

Q101.

Answer: D

Explanation: During a client consultation in nail services, noting any nail disorders, habits, or specific concerns is the main purpose of recording responses and observations.

Q102.

Answer: B

Explanation: Conditions like nail Beau's lines, onychomadesis and longitudinal melanonychia could prevent services while Leuconychia might restrict but not entirely prevent a service.

Q103.

Answer: B

Explanation: The cosmetologist would recommend shellac or gel polish to clients as it provides durability and chip-resistant nail color that lasts longer as compared to regular polish.

Q104.

Answer: C

Explanation: Maintaining a client record card helps in providing personalized services by recording preferences and service history.

Q105.

Answer. C

Explanation: During manicure, for adding shine and smooth wavy ridges on the natural nail, nail buffer is used.

Q106.

Answer. D

Explanation: Make sure precision for holding wooden pusher like a pencil in cuticle removal without damaging the nail plate, during manicure.

Q107.

Answer. A

Explanation: Please note that, cloudy disinfectant must be replaced to ensure effectiveness as it indicates contamination.

Q108.

Answer. C

Explanation: To take benefit most from the versatile and accommodating shoe cosmetologists are suggested with a broad range of clients and situations.

Q109.

Answer: C

Explanation: In French and American manicures, the aims of sheer color polish providing a natural appearance to the nails.

Q110.

Answer: C

Explanation: During an acrylic nail maintenance, smoothing the ledge prevents damage to the natural nail that ensures a safe and gentle process.

Cosmetology Exam Practice Test-3

Q1. To address the possible transmission of infections through shared cosmetic applicators. What specialized measures should cosmetologists used?

(A) Encouraging collaborative product usage

(B) Implementing routine equipment inspections

(C) Promoting single-use applicator adoption

(D) Enhancing salon aesthetics for infection prevention

Q2. As viruses rely on host cells for reproduction. What is the fundamental distinction between viruses and bacteria?

(A) Size

(B) Reproduction method

(C) Shape

(D) Color

Q3. HIV and hepatitis are bloodborne pathogens. What is the primary method of transmission through the body for them?

a) Airborne transmission

b) Saliva

c) Blood or body fluids

d) Skin-to-skin contact

Q4. If an exposure incident occurs, during a salon services. Which one of the following action is recommended?

(A) Continue the service

(B) Discard contaminated objects

(C) Clean the workstation late

(D) Avoid wearing gloves

Q5. In cosmetology, after disinfection. How implements should be treated?

(A) Seal them in an airtight container

(B) Store them in a damp environment

(C) Keep them exposed to air

(D) Rinse and dry thoroughly

Q6. In cosmetology, to prevent pathogen transmission among clients. How should cloth towels be handled?

(A) Wipe with a disinfectant

(B) Launder between each client

(C) Seal in an airtight container

(D) Reuse without cleaning

Q7. To prevent cross contamination between clients in salon. What is the best method as a cosmetologist?

(A) Sharing towels between clients

(B) Sterilizing tools once a week

(C) Storing tools in a moist environment

(D) Using single-use items or thoroughly cleaning multi-use tools

Q8. To uphold cosmetology standards. How does the use of disposable objects assist?

(A) By reducing salon expenses

(B) By promoting prolonged tool usage

(C) By ensuring salon tools remain moist

(D) By significantly lowering cross-contamination risks

Q9. During disposal to control infection, double bagging is recommended. The main purpose of double bagging of contaminated objects is:

(A) Enhance organization

(B) Reduce exposure risk

(C) Promote eco-friendly practices

(D) Increase efficiency

Q10. The sharp disposables, that come in contact with blood during an exposure incident. Which is the recommended method for disposing of them?

(A) Recycling

(B) Single-bagging

(C) Double-bagging

(D) Sharps box

Q11. In cosmetology industry, which federal agency regulates safety and health standards?

(A) Environmental Protection Agency (EPA)

(B) Food and Drug Administration (FDA)

(C) Occupational Safety and Health Administration (OSHA)

(D) Drug Enforcement Administration (DEA)

Q12. The practitioner has to cover the injury with an adhesive dressing in the salon. What should be the priority of the cosmetologist, after covering?

(A) Cleaning the workstation immediately.

(B) Placing all contaminated items in a trash container.

(C) Removing implements for disinfection.

(D) Placing gloves on both hands before continuing.

Q13. In salon, to ensure effective sanitation. The role of chelating detergents is:

(A) Removing visible debris

(B) Instant pathogen elimination

(C) Preventing mineral buildup

(D) Ensuring quick drying of surfaces

Q14. Before returning to service after addressing a bleeding injury incident. What essential precaution should a practitioner follow?

(A) Double-bag disposal of all contaminated items

(B) Application of an EPA-registered hospital disinfectant

(C) Donning new gloves and cleansing the hands thoroughly

(D) Implementing a full station decontamination procedure

Q15. What role does hair play, as a physical barrier on the scalp?

(A) UV protection

(B) Sensory perception

(C) Wound protection

(D) Sebum distribution

Q16. Which of the body's defenses against injury and bacterial invasion, is the main function of the skin?

(A) Excretion

(B) Sensation

(C) Heat regulation

(D) Protection

Q17. The visible part of the matrix under the living skin, often lighter in color, is called as:

(A) Cuticle

(B) Lunula

(C) Hyponychium

(D) Matrix bed

Q18. What genetically based factor causes hair loss in a specific pattern?

(A) Tinea capitis

(B) Androgenetic alopecia

(C) Alopecia areata

(D) Telogen effluvium

Q19. In a case of fungal infection, what causes hair breakage and often results in stubbled areas on the scalp?

(A) Tinea capitis

(B) Folliculitis

(C) Seborrheic dermatitis

(D) Pediculosis capitis

Q20. Which of the following ailment, could be often confused with contact dermatitis as itching and inflammation?

(A) Eczema

(B) Rosacea

(C) Hyperpigmentation

(D) Psoriasis

Q21. In which condition from the following, a series of lengthwise ridges on the nail plate appears to be rough?

(A) Plicatured nail

(B) Onychorrhexis

(C) Ridges

(D) Hangnail

Q22. Among the following options, which is the seventh cranial nerve?

(A) Trifacial nerve

(B) Ophthalmic nerve

(C) Facial nerve

(D) Zygomatic nerve

Q23. Which nerve provides sensation to the scalp, especially to the back of the neck?

(A) Greater occipital nerve

(B) Smaller occipital nerve

(C) Greater auricular nerve

(D) Cervical cutaneous nerve

Q24. From the following parts of neurons, which one receives impulses from neurons?

(A) Axon terminal

(B) Dendrite

(C) Cell body

(D) Nucleus

Q25. In what way does proper blood circulation impact skin complexion?

(A) Increases sebum production

(B) Improves skin elasticity

(C) Boosts collagen synthesis

(D) Determines eye color

Q26. How does blood circulation knowledge help in scalp treatments?

(A) Enhances nail polish adhesion

(B) Prevents skin discoloration

(C) Regulates hair coloring techniques

(D) Maximizes treatment effectiveness

Q27. Among the facial bones, which bone is the biggest and strongest?

(A) Zygomatic bone

(B) Maxilla bone

(C) Mandible

(D) Vomer bone

Q28. From the below mentioned, what structure articulates to form the shoulder joint with the Humerus?

(A) Clavicle

(B) Scapula

(C) Axilla

(D) Ribs

Q29. Considering the following options, which product is used for neutralizing hydroxide hair relaxers through acid-alkali neutralization reactions?

(A) Developer

(B) Shampoo

(C) Filler

(D) Normalizing lotion

Q30. Which of the following chemical reaction is the cause of chemical changes induced by hair colors and solutions used in permanent wave treatments?

(A) Combustion

(B) Oxidation–reduction

(C) Exothermic reaction

(D) Ionization

Q31. Concerning the formulation of emulsions, what is the main purpose of surfactants in cosmetic products?

(A) Increase acidity

(B) Create fragrance

(C) Emulsify oil and water

(D) Enhance color stability

Q32. Considering the importance of pH scale for cosmetologist, which of the following pH range shows an alkaline solution on the pH scale?

(A) 0-7

(B) 7

(C) 7-14

(D) 0

Q33. In a permanent wave formula, what is the main purpose of a reducing agent like thioglycolic acid?

(A) Increase hair volume

(B) Add shine to the hair

(C) Permanently change hair shape

(D) Strengthen hair roots

Q34. In hair relaxers, how does sodium hydroxide function work?

(A) Ammonium thioglycolate

(B) Sodium hydroxide

(C) Lithium hydroxide

(D) Hydrogen peroxide

Q35. What does the do cuticle for the hair shaft when properly overlapping?

(A) Adds color

(B) Locks in moisture

(C) Increases thickness

(D) Promotes growth

Q36. Considering the following options, for cosmetic formulation what is primary drawback to rely solely on pH test strips?

(A) Inaccuracy in color comparison

(B) Limited pH range coverage

(C) High cost

(D) Difficulty in handling

Q37. What is the chemical reaction with hydrogen peroxide in the process of hair bleaching?

(A) Melanin

(B) Titanium Dioxide

(C) Citric Acid

(D) Glycerin

Q38. By use of dihydroxyacetone (DHA), what chemical process occurs in skin darkening products?

(A) Oxidation

(B) Reduction

(C) Maillard reaction

(D) Polymerization

Q39. In the context which factor contributes to shiny hair?

(A) Dry scalp

(B) Well-functioning glands

(C) Lack of nutrients

(D) Dead hair follicles

Q40. To ensure client satisfaction, what step is essential before starting a return service?

(A) Confirm payment

(B) Quick consultation

(C) Schedule future appointments

(D) Update client records

Q41. A good shampoo and scalp massage what do provide for cosmetologists?

(A) Opportunity to shine

(B) Chance for artistic expression

(C) Platform for selling products

(D) Showcase of advanced techniques

Q42. To prevent the Pseudo folliculitis Barbae (PFB) what should be the direction for shaving?

(A) Against hair growth

(B) In the direction of hair growth

(C) Diagonally across hair growth

(D) Circular motion

Q43. What is the primary risk associated with neglecting the contraindications in cosmetology?

(A) Reduced client satisfaction

(B) Legal consequences

(C) Delayed treatment process

(D) Increased service variety

Q44. For a cosmetologist, why it is crucial to delay treatment for a client with conjunctivitis?

(A) To avoid allergic reactions

(B) To prevent compensation claims

(C) Due to its contagious nature

(D) To save time and resources

Q45. In hair services, what is the primary purpose of strand testing?

(A) Scalp massage

(B) Hair straightening

(C) Assessing color results

(D) Nail care

Q46. What type of alopecia is best assessed by a family physician and can be diagnosed clinically and treated with minoxidil?

(A) Scarring alopecia

(B) Androgenetic alopecia

(C) Tinea capitis

(D) Trichotillomania

Q47. In female pattern hair loss, what term describes the miniaturization of scalp hairs?

(A) Follicular transformation

(B) Hair elongation

(C) Hair miniaturization

(D) Scalp involution

Q48. In the treatment of lichen planopilaris, which diabetes medication, beneficial for primary cicatricial scarring alopecia?

(A) Metformin

(B) Insulin

(C) Pioglitazone

(D) Glipizide

Q49. In the context of dandruff leading to peeling and flaking of the scalp skin, what is the primary cause of dandruff?

(A) Poor Hygiene

(B) Excess Sebum

(C) Dry Scalp

(D) Fungal Infection

Q50. During or at the end of a treatment in the client record, what is the purpose of recording anything unexpected?

(A) Emergency contact details

(B) Compliance with laws

(C) Treatment specifics

(D) Results of treatment

Q51. In cosmetology, what is the primary objective of using hair rollers with a 0.8-inch diameter?

(A) Straighten hair

(B) Add volume

(C) Create small curls

(D) Achieve a wet set

Q52. In cosmetology, what is the key purpose of using a professional hood dryer?

(A) Create curls

(B) Set wet hairstyles

(C) Straighten hair

(D) Add shine

Q53. What is the reason behind using a specialized barber chair in cosmetology work?

(A) Enhance hair growth

(B) Ensure client comfort

(C) Control client position

(D) Minimize expenses

Q54. In cosmetology settings, how does the proper use of capes contribute to infection control procedures?

(A) Enhancing salon aesthetics

(B) Minimizing salon costs

(C) Preventing cross-contamination

(D) Improving stylist comfort

Q55. According to safety and infection control practices, how should brushes and combs be cleaned after each use?

(A) Wash with soap

(B) Rinse with water

(C) Follow manufacturer's directions

(D) Disinfect with hospital-level spray

Q56. In cosmetology, how crimping iron differ in function from a curling iron?

A) Adds shine to the hair

B) Achieves closer cuts

C) Creates textured styles

D) Precision sectioning

Q57. In cosmetology, what is the importance of disinfecting clipper blades with an EPA-registered, hospital-level disinfectant spray?

A) Adds shine to the hair

B) Precision cutting

C) Ensures hygiene and safety

D) Achieves closer cuts

Q58. Which of the following statements accurately describes the function of a barrette in hairstyling within cosmetology?

A) Adds shine to the hair

B) Used for hair separation during cutting

C) Creates volume

D) Secures hair in place

Q59. In cosmetology, which material is commonly used for disposable neck strips, ensuring single-use for each client?

A) Paper

B) Linen

C) Terry cloth

D) Microfiber

Q60. According to Ergonomic concepts, what is the significance of proper posture in salon?

A) Enhances client comfort

B) Ensures hygiene and safety

C) Facilitates hair color absorption

D) Prevents musculoskeletal disorders

Q61. During a service in the salon, how should a cosmetologist handle tools dropped on the floor?

(A) Leave them on the floor until the service is completed

(B) Discard them immediately

(C) Remove, clean, and disinfect or sterilize them

(D) Place them in pockets for later use

Q62. In addition to grooming facial hair, what does a hair clipper assist with in cosmetology settings?

(A) Straightening hair

(B) Creating curls

(C) Trimming bangs

(D) Adding volume

Q63. Being gentler on hair fiber's health, what attributes contribute to sulfate free shampoo?

(A) It enhances color

(B) It focuses on deep conditioning

(C) It lacks anionic surfactants

(D) It contains special additives

Q64. For hydrating and conditioning the skin, what natural ingredient is specifically selected for its dual benefits?

(A) Chamomile

(B) Aloe Vera

(C) Coconut Oil

(D) Jojoba Oil

Q65. Which movement employs both gentle stroking and circular hand motions to induce relaxation in massage techniques?

(A) Petrissage

(B) Tapotement

(C) Effleurage

(D) Friction

Q66. Which technique is commonly employed for providing a relaxing scalp massage in the context of scalp treatment?

(A) Tapping

(B) Kneading

(C) Friction

(D) Effleurage

Q67. What specific aspect should stylists assess and address for optimal client care in chemical draping?

(A) Hair color

(B) Dryness and replace towels if necessary

(C) Styling preferences

(D) Jewelry damage

Q68. In draping procedure, what material is frequently employed for neck strips to ensure absorbency and comfort of the client?

(A) Plastic

(B) Paper

(C) Cloth

(D) Metal

Q69. Which specific classification possesses heat resistance and is characterized by a glossy appearance?

(A) Type 1 - Straight

(B) Type 2 - Wavy

(C) Type 3 - Curly

(D) Type 4 - Coily/Kinky

Q70. What specific attribute shows variation distinguishing its unique characteristics in the realm of Type 3A curly hair?

(A) Curl definition

(B) Volume

(C) Coarseness

(D) Shine

Q71. In the context of hair design, what is the danger of confining stylists to the basics?

(A) Lack of creativity

(B) Increased satisfaction

(C) Improved safety

(D) Better client relationships

Q72. When choosing a haircut for a client with naturally curly hair, what should a hairstylist consider?

(A) Straight styles

(B) Soft and wispy cuts

(C) Analyzing hair density

(D) Emphasizing jawlines

Q73. During a hair cutting, what is the main purpose of sectioning clips?

(A) Detangle hair

(B) Section and subsection hair

(C) Create crisp outlines

(D) Remove bulk from hair

Q74. In the context of hairstyling, what is the main purpose of a client consultation?

(A) Entertainment

(B) Advertisement

(C) Communication

(D) Evaluation

Q75. Which of the following is particularly beneficial for thermal curling with an electric iron?

(A) Curly hair with rollers

(B) Straight hair without rollers

(C) Extremely curly hair

(D) Wet hair

Q76. Before braiding, why is it important to analyze the health of the scalp?

(A) Ensure even drying

(B) Prevent breakage

(C) Avoid scalp damage

(D) Enhance curl pattern

Q77. In cosmetology, what is the difference between a hairpiece and a wig?

(A) Size

(B) Color

(C) Texture

(D) Coverage

Q78. Which one is associated with the characteristics of integration hairpieces, among the following options?

(A) Attached with tape

(B) Heavy and bulky

(C) Lightweight and natural-looking

(D) Worn to sleep at night

Q79. When cutting a wig for a more realistic look, what should be the primary goal of a cosmetologist?

(A) Solid shape

(B) Tapered ends

(C) Blunt cut

(D) Layered texture

Q80. In the processing of which permanent wave is it necessary to utilize an external heat source?

(A) Exothermic waves

(B) Acid waves

(C) Alkaline waves

(D) Endothermic waves

Q81. What is the natural pH range of hair? Please select one from the following.

(A) 2.5-3.5

(B) 4.5-5.5

(C) 6.0-7.0

(D) 8.0-9.0

Q82. During color processing, what characterizes hair with high porosity?

(A) Slower color uptake

(B) Quick color uptake

(C) Dense cuticle

(D) Minimal color fading

Q83. Before the preliminary strand test during lightening, what should be checked about 15 minutes?

(A) Color application

(B) Cotton placement

(C) Lightening action

(D) Strand test

Q84. What makes hair treated with hydroxide relaxers unsuitable for permanent waving?

(A) Increased volume

(B) Enhanced curls

(C) Lanthionization process

(D) Disulfide bonds cannot reform

Q85. How do Keratin straightening treatments work on the hair?

(A) Break bonds

(B) Fix keratin in place

(C) Deactivate alkaline residues

(D) Rebuild disulfide bonds

Q86. In creating a successful permanent wave what is the key factor?

(A) Rod size

(B) Wrapping technique

(C) End paper color

(D) Hair thickness

Q87. What is the primary protein that makes up hair strands?

(A) Collagen

(B) Keratin

(C) Elastin

(D) Melanin

Q88. In hair structure, which layer is primarily responsible for the majority of pigment and strength?

(A) Cuticle

(B) Cortex

(C) Medulla

(D) Follicle

Q89. Considering the following options, where should a cosmetologist highlight important observations in a client's treatment record?

(A) On the client's face

(B) In the treatment room

(C) With a color pen

(D) On the consultation card

Q90. From the given option, what is the primary function of the skin when you are hot?

(A) Constrict blood vessels

(B) Sweat and dilate blood vessels

(C) Produce vitamin D

(D) Form a defensive barrier

Q91. From the following option, why cosmetologists should scarring less than 6 months old be considered before giving beauty treatments?

(A) To prevent scarring

(B) To avoid compensation claims

(C) To limit treatment options

(D) To ensure proper healing

Q92. From the given option, what describes that Gua Sha differ from the Jade Roller in its application?

(A) Gua Sha reduces puffiness

(B) Jade Roller increases collagen production

(C) Gua Sha is a massage technique

(D) Jade Roller is made of semi-precious stone

Q93. From the following options, which substance is a common cause of acne and released by sebaceous glands?

(A) Collagen

(B) Elastin

(C) Sebum

(D) Keratin

Q94. In the context of cosmetology, what is the relation of ergonomics?

(A) Hair growth

(B) Workplace design

(C) Nail art techniques

(D) Makeup application

Q95. In the context of infection control standards, what must be virucidal, fungicidal, and bactericidal?

(A) Towels

(B) Disinfectants

(C) Shampoos

(D) Moisturizers

Q96. From the following option, what is the purpose of utilizing effleurage at the beginning and end of a massage?

(A) Relaxation

(B) Circulation

(C) Stimulation

(D) Toning

Q97. In the context of effective hair removal, which of the following condition must be met?

(A) Lighter hair than surrounding skin

(B) Recent chemical peel

(C) Use of Retin-A

(D) Presence of pustules

Q98. Along with color and hairstyles, what role does makeup play in cosmetology?

(A) Complex transformations

(B) Simple concealment

(C) Psychological enhancement

(D) Minimal impact

Q99. In order to treat redness and aging in light therapy, which type of light is normally used?

(A) Blue light

(B) Infrared light

(C) Green light

(D) Red light

Q100. During client consultation, what is the importance of discussing a client's expectations?

(A) Accelerating service time

(B) Demonstrating expertise

(C) Ensuring client satisfaction

(D) Reducing service cost

Q101. Regarding enhancements, what information should be recorded for nail services during a client consultation?

(A) Client's hair coloring history

(B) Notes on preferred massage techniques

(C) Performance assessment of the enhancements

(D) Details about scalp health conditions

Q102. Considering the following options, which conditions would generally prevent the provision of a nail service during consultation?

(A) Hangnail

(B) Nail ridges

(C) Tinea corporis

(D) Beau's lines

Q103. For a client with sensitive skin prone to nail polish allergies, considering the following options what should you recommend?

(A) Hypoallergenic nail polish

(B) Nail strengthening treatments

(C) Nail extension services

(D) Matte finish topcoat

Q104. In a salon setting, when should a cosmetologist update a client's service history in their records? In view of above please choose the right answer.

(A) After every salon staff meeting

(B) Solely on the client's birthday

(C) Post each concluded salon service session

(D) On a quarterly basis

Q105. For trimming toenails which tool is used and may have a miniature file attached?

(A) Nail scissors

(B) Toenail clippers

(C) Cuticle pusher

(D) Nail buffer

Q106. After being removed from the disinfectant solution how should implements be dried?

(A) Wipe with a dry cloth

(B) Let air dry

(C) Blow dry with a fan

(D) Rinse with warm water

Q107. To store the clean and disinfected abrasives, what is the preferred material?

(A) Plastic bag

(B) Sealed container

(C) Clean, unsealed container

(D) Airtight container

Q108. In nail care profession, what is the proposed solution for improving ergonomics according to the text?

(A) Introducing more temporary accommodations

(B) Using heavy salon equipment

(C) Implementing better posture at the nail station

(D) Ignoring ergonomic challenges

Q109. Which of the following step ensures the best adhesion of polish to the nail plate according to the cosmetologists?

(A) Applying lotion

(B) Using a high-shine buffer

(C) Cleaning under the free edge

(D) Brushing the nails

Q110. During an acrylic nail rebalance process, what must be used to remove existing polish?

(A) Cotton-tipped wooden pusher

(B) Fine buffer (350 grit)

(C) Medium-coarse abrasive (120 to 180 grit)

(D) High-shine buffer

Test 3 Answer Key

Q1.

Answer: C

Explanation: To minimize the risk of infection transmission in cosmetology. The specific infection control measure is utilization of single-use applicators.

Q2.

Answer: B

Explanation: Bacteria can live and reproduce independently. On the other hand, viruses reproduce by penetrating other cells.

Q3.

Answer: C

Explanation: As bloodborne pathogens pose a risk during salon services. Please note that, they are transmitted to the body in blood or body fluids.

Q4.

Answer: B

Explanation: If an exposure incident occurs, it is necessary to follow safety procedures. For example, cleaning the injured area and discarding contaminated objects.

Q5.

Answer: D

Explanation: In cosmetology, it is important to maintain cleanliness and prevent microbial growth during storage. After disinfection, implements should be cleaned properly by rinsing, followed by thorough drying.

Q6.

Answer: B

Explanation: To prevent pathogen transmission between clients during services. Cloth towels in cosmetology should be laundered to ensure client hygiene.

Q7.

Answer: D

Explanation: To minimize the risk of cross-contamination between clients. Please note that either use single-use items or thoroughly clean multi-use tools.

Q8.

Answer: D

Explanation: The use of disposable items aligns with cosmetology standards to prioritise hygiene and client safety. Kindly note that disposable objects significantly lower cross-contamination risks.

Q9.

Answer: B

Explanation: In the salon, during disposal, double bagging contributes to effective infection control. It also minimizes the danger of exposure in salon settings.

Q10.

Answer: D

Explanation: In cosmetology, disposing of sharp disposables in sharps box ensures proper containment. Please note that, sharps box disposing method also reduces the danger of injury.

Q11.

Answer: C

Explanation: Since OSHA is the federal authority responsible for maintaining safety and health standards in all workplaces. Likewise, it upholds health standards in cosmetology industry.

Q12.

Answer: C

Explanation: To prevent additional contamination in the workspace and ensure hygiene standards. Firstly, the practitioner's injury is addressed by an adhesive dressing, and then implements are removed from the site of the injury.

Q13.

Answer: C

Explanation: To ensure effective sanitation after spa, in salon. Please note that chelating detergents help prevent mineral buildup in foot spas.

Q14.

Answer: C

Explanation: In the case of a post-bleeding, before returning to the service the practitioners have to take preventive measures to stop contamination spread. These preventive measures include personal hygiene with new gloves and hand cleansing.

Q15.

Answer: C

Explanation: Hair acts as a physical barrier, which protects the scalp from the weather and protects against injuries or wounds.

Q16.

Answer: D

Explanation: The main role of the skin is to protect the body from injuries and bacterial invasion, functioning as an important barrier of defense against external risks to general health.

Q17.

Answer: B

Explanation: The visible part of the matrix under the skin is known as the lunula, which shows the true color of the matrix.

Q18.

Answer: B

Explanation: A particular pattern of hair loss caused by genetics is seen in androgenetic alopecia.

Q19.

Answer: A

Explanation: Tinea capitis is a fungal infection, which causes hair breakage and stubbled areas on the scalp.

Q20.

Answer: A

Explanation: Eczema can often be confused with contact dermatitis, as itching and inflammation are present in common.

Q21.

Answer: B

Explanation: Onychorrhexis is the condition, which may results in rough, split nails with lengthwise ridges. It can happen due to matrix injury.

Q22.

Answer: C

Explanation: The seventh cranial nerve is known as the facial nerve, and is mainly responsible for the facial expressions and sensation.

Q23.

Answer: D

Explanation: The cervical cutaneous nerve gives sensation to the scalp, mostly affecting the back of the neck area.

Q24.

Answer: B

Explanation: Dendrites are the parts of neurons, which receive impulses from other neurons. They help in communication within the nervous system.

Q25.

Answer: B

Explanation: Proper blood circulation improves skin elasticity, by delivering oxygen and nutrients. It helps in maintaining skin health, which leads to a youthful complexion.

Q26.

Answer: D

Explanation: In scalp treatments, understanding blood circulation is very important. It helps in increasing the effectiveness of various treatments targeted for scalp health.

Q27.

Answer: C

Explanation: The mandible is the largest and strongest bone in the face. It offers support and structure to the lower part of the face.

Q28.

Answer: B

Explanation: The scapula articulates with the Humerus to form the shoulder joint. It helps in arm movement and gives stability within the shoulder complex.

Q29.

Answer: D

Explanation: To neutralize hydroxide hair relaxers, normalizing lotions are used. They provide hair safety by creating an acid-alkali neutralization reaction.

Q30.

Answer: B

Explanation: Oxidation-reduction reactions are the cause of chemical changes in permanent waves, hair colors and, related services.

Q31.

Answer: C

Explanation: In cosmetic products, please note that the main purpose of surfactants is to emulsify oil and water to form stable emulsions.

Q32.

Answer: C

Explanation: The pH of alkaline solution is above 7 and cosmetologists should be aware of the implications for hair and skin, understanding the importance of pH scale.

Q33.

Answer: C

Explanation: In a permanent wave, thioglycolic acid permanently changes hair shape by reacting with di-sulfur bonds.

Q34.

Answer: B

Explanation: For facilitating the straightening process in hair relaxers, sodium hydroxide breaks di-sulfur bonds in curly hair.

Q35.

Answer: B

Explanation: Within the hair shaft, overlapping cuticle scales locks in moisture that providing protection and a smooth appearance.

Q36.

Answer: B

Explanation: In the specific pH ranges, pH test have limited coverage making them less precise for detailed cosmetic formulation.

Q37.

Answer: A

Explanation: As described in the question, in the process of hair bleaching involves a chemical reaction between melanin and hydrogen peroxide.

Q38.

Answer: C

Explanation: Through the Maillard reaction, DHA reacts with skin proteins that produce a brown color, creating the appearance of a tan.

Q39.

Answer: B

Explanation: Crucial for the shine and health of the hair, well-functioning glands on the scalp are responsible for producing natural oils.

Q40.

Answer: B

Explanation: Before return services, a quick consultation prevents misunderstandings and maintains client satisfaction.

Q41.

Answer: A

Explanation: By properly performing a shampoo and scalp massage, cosmetologists are provided with an opportunity to shine in delivering quality service and ensuring client satisfaction.

Q42.

Answer: B

Explanation: Shaving in the direction of hair growth is recommended because it prevents PFB and ingrown hairs.

Q43.

Answer: B

Explanation: In cosmetology, ignoring contraindications can lead to legal consequences, emphasizing the importance of thorough assessment for client safety and compliance.

Q44.

Answer: C

Explanation: In the salon environment, to prevent the spread of infection. It is crucial to delay treatment for conjunctivitis.

Q45.

Answer: C

Explanation: In hair services, the primary purpose of strand testing is assessing and achieving desired hair color results.

Q46.

Answer: B

Explanation: Clinically diagnosed and treated with minoxidil, and family physicians handle the assessment of androgenetic alopecia.

Q47.

Answer: C

Explanation: In female pattern hair loss, it involves the miniaturization of scalp hairs, resulting in finer and thinner versions.

Q48.

Answer: C

Explanation: The diabetes medication pioglitazone is considered for treating lichen planopilaris, a scarring alopecia. Its anti-inflammatory effects can help manage this inflammatory hair loss condition effectively.

Q49.

Answer: C

Explanation: Peeling and flaking of the scalp, caused by dandruff, is primarily due to a dry scalp condition, leading to the shedding of skin flakes.

Q50.

Answer: C

Explanation: During or after a treatment recording unexpected occurrences provides important details for treatment specifics in the client record.

Q51.

Answer: C

Explanation: Cosmetologists often use hair rollers with a 0.8-inch diameter to create small curls in hairs.

Q52.

Answer: B

Explanation: Cosmetologists use Professional hood dryers for setting wet hairstyles, and enhancing the styling process.

Q53.

Answer: C

Explanation: By using a specialized barber chair, cosmetologists can control client's position and facilitate the work without straining.

Q54.

Answer: C

Explanation: In cosmetology settings, the proper use of capes is essential to prevent cross-contamination, infection control, and maintain a hygienic salon environment.

Q55.

Answer: C

Explanation: According to safety and infection control practices, brushes and combs should be cleaned by following manufacturer's directions after each use.

Q56.

Answer: C

Explanation: Cosmetologists use crimping irons to create textured styles that provide a unique pattern compared to the curls produced by curling irons.

Q57.

Answer: C

Explanation: In cosmetology settings, disinfecting clipper blades with an EPA-registered, hospital-level disinfectant spray ensures hygiene and safety.

Q58.

Answer: D

Explanation: In cosmetology settings, barrettes are used to secure hair in place during hairstyling.

Q59.

Answer: A

Explanation: Disposable neck strips used in salon services are commonly made of paper to ensure single-use for each client, and promote infection control in cosmetology.

Q60.

Answer: D

Explanation: According to ergonomic concepts, proper posture in salon prevents cosmetologists from musculoskeletal disorders. It ensures the well-being of cosmetologists throughout their careers.

Q61.

Answer: C

Explanation: It is recommended to remove, clean, and disinfect or sterilize the tools dropped on the floor during a service in cosmetology before further use.

Q62.

Answer: C

Explanation: Apart from grooming facial hair, hair clippers assist to trim bangs and provide precision in creating various lengths and styles.

Q63.

Answer: C

Explanation: Ensuring a gentler cleansing action for hair fiber health sulfate free shampoo are considered milder as they omit anionic surfactants.

Q64.

Answer: B

Explanation: Making it a preferred natural ingredient in skincare formulations, Aloe Vera stands out for its skin hydrating and conditioning properties.

Q65.

Answer: C

Explanation: Promoting scalp health through its gentle application, effleurage utilizes soothing stroking movements, fostering relaxation.

Q66.

Answer: D

Explanation: For delivering a soothing scalp massage during a Scalp Treatment, effleurage stands out as a frequently used technique.

Q67.

Answer: B

Explanation: During chemical draping to ensure client comfort and safety stylists should diligently check for dryness and promptly replace towels if necessary.

Q68.

Answer: B

Explanation: During draping procedure to prioritize client's comfort and functionality neck strips are commonly used and crafted from absorbent paper or cloth.

Q69.

Answer: A

Explanation Distinguishing its unique characteristics, Type 1 Straight hair exhibits both heat resistance and a naturally glossy appearance.

Q70.

Answer: C

Explanation: Contributing to the distinctive nature of this particular curl pattern, Type 3A hair displays diversity in coarseness.

Q71.

Answer: A

Explanation: In the above context, the danger of confining stylists to the basics is evident. Playing it safe can lead to dull and repetitive hairstyles, limiting creativity.

Q72.

Answer: C

Explanation: When choosing a haircut for a client with naturally curly hair make sure the haircut suits the client's hair type. And analyzing curly hair involves considering density and texture.

Q73.

Answer: B

Explanation: During the hair cutting process. The main purpose of sectioning clips is to section and subsection the hair.

Q74.

Answer: C

Explanation: The primary goal of a client consultation in hairstyling is communication. It aims to ensure effective communication to understand preferences and consider face shape, hair type, and lifestyle.

Q75.

Answer: B

Explanation: Thermal curling with an electric iron is especially beneficial for eliminating the need for rollers on straight hair. And electric thermal curling is useful for quick styling.

Q76.

Answer: C

Explanation: In this context, it is very important to analyze the scalp health before braiding. To ensure that the scalp is healthy and properly cared for during braiding.

Q77.

Answer: D

Explanation: In cosmetology, a wig provide a 100 percent coverage on the head. And a hairpiece is a short wig that only covers the top or crown of the head.

Q78.

Answer: C

Explanation: Integration hairpieces effortlessly blend with the client's own hair, and are lightweight and natural-looking in appearance.

Q79.

Answer: B

Explanation: A cosmetologist should focus on tapering the ends when cutting a wig to achieve a more natural look, avoiding a solid unnatural shape.

Q80.

Answer: D

Explanation: Endothermic waves absorb heat from an external source for processing.

Q81.

Answer: B

Explanation: The natural pH of hair falls between 4.5 and 5.5.

Q82.

Answer: B

Explanation: Highly porous hair takes color quickly but may also experience faster color fading.

Q83.

Answer: C

Explanation: Check for the progress of lightening about 15 minutes before the expected time.

Q84.

Answer: D

Explanation: The lanthionization process in hydroxide relaxers prevents disulfide bonds from reforming for permanent waving.

Q85.

Answer: B

Explanation: Keratin treatments work by fixing keratin in place; they do not break bonds.

Q86.

Answer: B

Explanation: The correct perm rod and wrapping method are crucial for success.

Q87.

Answer: B

Explanation: Keratin forms the structural basis of hair.

Q88.

Answer: B

Explanation: In the view of above, cortex holds pigment & provides strength to the hair.

Q89.

Answer: C

Explanation: Highlighting important observations with a color pen in the treatment record ensures attention to critical details for personalized skincare.

Q90.

Answer: B

Explanation: Please note that when we are hot, the main function of the skin is to cool the body by sweating and dilating blood vessels, regulating temperature.

Q91.

Answer: C

Explanation: In order to support proper healing, fresh scarring should not be stressed, limiting beauty treatments in the affected area.

Q92.

Answer: C

Explanation: Please note that Jade Roller is specifically created for facial massage, promoting collagen production and reducing tension, while Gua Sha uses a facial scrapping massage technique.

Q93.

Answer: C

Explanation: Please note that sebum is an oily substance that can contribute to acne when trapped in folicles, necessitating effective skincare practices.

Q94.

Answer: B

Explanation: In the context of cosmetology, Ergonomics is about optimizing workplace design to foster comfort, efficiency and safety, preventing musculoskeletal disorders among professionals.

Q95.

Answer: B

Explanation: Please note that in order to effectively kill potentially infectious bacteria, disinfectants used in salons must be fungicidal, virucidal, and bactericidal, ensuring a safe salon environment.

Q96.

Answer: A

Explanation: Promoting overall relaxation, effleurage is used for relaxing and soothing effects at the start and end of a massage.

Q97.

Answer: A

Explanation: Please note that when the hair is lighter than the surrounding skin, laser hair removal is most effective.

Q98.

Answer: C

Explanation: Along with color and hairstyles makeup helps clients to achieve psychosocial enhancement and beautiful changes, boosting confidence and overall appearance.

Q99.

Answer: D

Explanation: In order to treat aging and redness, red light is normally used in light therapy, promoting overall skin improvement and overall production.

Q100.

Answer: C

Explanation: Ensuring satisfaction and meeting client needs are essential when discussing a client's expectations during consultation.

Q101.

Answer: C

Explanation: During client consultation for nail services, performance assessment of the enhancements should be recorded regarding enhancements.

Q102.

Answer: C

Explanation: During nail consultation, due to its infectious nature a body ringworm tinea corporis prohibits nail services, requiring referral to a doctor for treatment.

Q103.

Answer: A

Explanation: For individuals with sensitive skin, please note that hypoallergenic nail polishes are formulated to minimize the risk of allergic reactions and are best recommendation.

Q104.

Answer: C

Explanation: To maintain precise and current records, a cosmetologist should update a client's service history in their record after every concluded salon service session.

Q105.

Answer. B

Explanation: Please note that, toenail clippers are used to trim toenails and may have a miniature file attached for manicuring.

Q106.

Answer. B

Explanation: To prevent from rusting, implements should be rinsed well in water and allowed to air dry after removal.

Q107.

Answer. C

Explanation: To prevent bacterial growth and contamination it is recommended to store clean and disinfected abrasives in a clean, unsealed container.

Q108.

Answer. C

Explanation: To improve ergonomics in the nail care profession, the cosmetologists suggest better posture at the nail station as a solution.

Q109.

Answer. C

Explanation: To ensure optimal adhesion of polish to the nail plate cleaning under the free edge removes debris.

Q110.

Answer: C

Explanation: By using a medium-coarse abrasive (120 to 180 grit) to prepare for maintenance steps existing polish is removed during rebalancing.

Cosmetology Exam Practice Test-4

Q1. In the context of infection control, prevention of the spread of infections is emphasized in cosmetology. Why?

(A) To reduce tool wear

(B) To ensure client comfort

(C) To fulfill legal obligations

(D) To save on disinfectant costs

Q2. In salon settings, which is the primary cause of bacterial infections, among the following options?

(A) Fungal pathogens

(B) Viral agents

(C) Parasitic organisms

(D) Pathogenic bacteria

Q3. In barbering practices, for the eradication of the danger of HIV transmission. Which one of the following, is the most effective method?

(A) Mandatory minimum equipment standards

(B) Disposable sharp instruments

(C) Standardized disinfection and sterilization

(D) Increasing service prices

Q4. A process that eradicates many or all pathogenic microorganisms on inanimate objects. Which terminology is used for this process?

(A) Sterilization

(B) Cleaning

(C) Disinfection

(D) Decontamination

Q5. For cosmetology implements, what is the recommended post-disinfection?

(A) Encase them in an airtight container

(B) Immerse in a humid environment

(C) Expose them to circulating air

(D) Rinse and dry meticulously

Q6. In cosmetology, for foot spa cleaning, chelating detergent is used. What is the primary purpose of its utilization in cleaning?

(A) Enhance fragrance

(B) Remove visible debris

(C) Increase foaming

(D) Disinfect surfaces

Q7. In a salon setting, to prevent cross contamination. Which one of the following practices contributes most?

(A) Storing tools without cleaning between clients

(B) Cleaning tools with water only

(C) Sterilizing tools monthly

(D) Sanitizing tools between clients

Q8. By transferring microorganisms to a handler. Which practice leads to cross contamination?

(A) Direct contact with clients

(B) Handling contaminated towels

(C) Frequent sanitation of tools

(D) Use of single-use items

Q9. When utilizing disinfecting products in a salon setting. The instructions such as contact time, surface type, and mixing are important to follow. Why?

(A) Enhance product effectiveness

(B) Save time

(C) Improve salon ambiance

(D) Comply with federal law

Q10. The main role of the EPA in cosmetology is to license disinfectants. What other role can the EPA serve in this field?

(A) Dictating beauty product formulations

(B) Approving salon interior designs

(C) Monitoring cosmetologist dress codes

(D) Establishing environmental impact guidelines

Q11. For salon products, which information is commonly included in the Material Safety Data Sheet?

(A) Product price

(B) Safe handling procedures

(C) Customer reviews

(D) Stylist recommendations

Q12. During a practitioner's injury, after placing contaminated objects in a properly marked double bag. As a cosmetologist, what should do next?

(A) Proceed with the service using gloves.

(B) Replace gloves and continue working.

(C) Clean affected surfaces and implements.

(D) Apply an antiseptic with bare hands.

Q13. During the cleaning process, in the salon. What is the main purpose of an ultrasonic unit?

(A) Aesthetics

(B) Disinfection

(C) Removing visible debris

(D) Enhancing client comfort

Q14. When treating the blood exposure injury of a practitioner. Which one of the following actions best exemplifies compliance with safety standards?

(A) Immediate disposal of contaminated gloves in double bags

(B) Utilization of an aseptic technique during wound care

(C) Application of a specialized wound-healing gel

(D) Excusing oneself and cleaning the workstation surfaces

Q15. Which part of the hair follicle contains the dermal papilla, and is essential for hair growth?

(A) Hair bulb

(B) Follicle infundibulum

(C) Suprabulbar region

(D) Upper isthmus

Q16. Which gland aids in controlling the temperature by excreting perspiration through the skin from the following?

(A) Sebaceous gland

(B) Sweat gland

(C) Oil gland

(D) Hair follicle

Q17. Which tissue from the following forms the barrier to prevent the invasion of foreign materials and microorganisms between the natural plate and living skin?

(A) Hyponychium

(B) Matrix

(C) Cuticle

(D) Nail bed

Q18. Which scalp condition involves redness, itching, and oily, yellowish scales from the following?

(A) Tinea capitis

(B) Seborrheic dermatitis

(C) Telogen effluvium

(D) Trichotillomania

Q19. The hair loss that occurs due to an allergic reaction to specific hair products, which scalp disorder is involved?

(A) Seborrheic dermatitis

(B) Contact dermatitis

(C) Androgenetic alopecia

(D) Alopecia areata

Q20. What can aid in dead skin cell removal and prevent clogged pores and skin issues, from the following?

(A) Exfoliation

(B) Hyperpigmentation

(C) Inflammation

(D) Acne

Q21. Due to poor circulation, which term is used for nails turning into different colors?

(A) Discolored nails

(B) Nail pterygium

(C) Pincer nail

(D) Splinter hemorrhages

Q22. Which nerve affects the skin above the temple, up to the top of the skull, from the following?

(A) Supraorbital nerve

(B) Infraorbital nerve

(C) Auriculotemporal nerve

(D) Infratrochlear nerve

Q23. What is the primary structural unit of the nervous system from the following?

(A) Neuron

(B) Dendrite

(C) Axon terminal

(D) Nerve fiber

Q24. Which nervous system's division is responsible for involuntary muscle control from the following?

(A) Central nervous system

(B) Peripheral nervous system

(C) Autonomic nervous system

(D) Sensory nervous system

Q25. How does the circulatory system impact nail care?

(A) Determines skin hydration levels

(B) Influences hair texture

(C) Regulates nail growth rate

(D) Enhances makeup application

Q26. Why is knowledge of blood circulation important for chemical treatments?

(A) Influences nail polish durability

(B) Prevents scalp dryness

(C) Aids in hair color selection

(D) Reduces risks during procedures

Q27. In cosmetology studies, the structure of foot is made up of how many bones?

(A) 24

(B) 26

(C) 28

(D) 30

Q28. Which bone is articulated with the femur to form the hip joint?

(A) Pelvis

(B) Sacrum

(C) Coccyx

(D) Ilium

Q29. How are water droplets positioned and how do they affect the feel of the emulsion in a water-in-oil emulsion?

(A) Externally; less greasy

(B) Internally; less greasy

(C) Externally; more greasy

(D) Internally; more greasy

Q30. For the skin and imparts shine which common cosmetic ingredient functions as a water resistant lubricant to hair?

(A) Glycerin

(B) Silicones

(C) Alkanolamines

(D) Volatile alcohols

Q31. During the oxidation of hair color or the polymerization of acrylic nail enhancements, what kind of chemical change occurs?

(A) Exothermic

(B) Endothermic

(C) Physical

(D) Neutralization

Q32. What defines the combined properties of the substances involved in a physical mixture?

(A) Solubility

(B) Solute

(C) Solvent

(D) Emulsifier

Q33. In the hair bleaching procedure, what kind of chemical process involves?

(A) Oxidation of melanin with ammonia

(B) Reduction of hydrogen peroxide with cystine

(C) Reaction of di-sulfur bonds with thioglycolic acid

(D) Oxidation of melanin with hydrogen peroxide

Q34. In the context of permanently changing hair shape in products like permanent waves, which of the following chemical process is crucial?

(A) Oxidation

(B) Ion exchange

(C) Acid-base reaction

(D) Reduction of di-sulfur bonds

Q35. From the following options, long hair can be affected by constant opening and closing of the cuticle caused by soap-based products. How does this process damage the long hair?

(A) Enhances growth

(B) Adds volume

(C) Causes irreparable damage

(D) Promotes shine

Q36. Despite its higher cost, what factors could lead a person to choose a pH meter for cosmetic formulation?

(A) Longer lifespan

(B) Vibrant color readings

(C) No calibration required

(D) Suitable for non-aqueous products

Q37. In nail care products what is the main purpose of toluene?

(A) Add fragrance

(B) Improve texture

(C) Dissolve substances

(D) Provide color

Q38. To change the shape of hair permanently which of the following cosmetic product is specifically designed?

(A) Hair Relaxer

(B) Hair Bleach

(C) Permanent Waves

(D) Hair Colors

Q39. If a client wants a level 9 but hair can only safely lift to level 7 then what should you do?

(A) Use a stronger product

(B) Choose an alternative goal

(C) Apply a scalp treatment

(D) Skip the strand test

Q40. When lifting artificial color, what does a strand test reveal?

(A) Hair thickness

(B) Even lifting

(C) Scalp sensitivity

(D) Cuticle health

Q41. For cosmetologists, why it is essential to be a good listener?

(A) Demonstrates indifference

(B) Validates product choices

(C) Enhances artistic skills

(D) Facilitates strong relationships

Q42. Caused by oily hair products, what effectively treats pomade scalp acne?

(A) Tea tree oil

(B) Salicylic acid

(C) Coconut oil

(D) Cocoa butter

Q43. In dealing with relative contraindication, what crucial role does a doctor's note play?

(A) Exclusion

(B) Modification

(C) Approval

(D) Confirmation

Q44. If a client presents with undiagnosed swelling and facial lumps when is it appropriate for a cosmetologist to delay treatment for a client?

(A) Always

(B) Only if visible

(C) Never

(D) Only if requested

Q45. For porosity assessment, in what situation should you conduct a strand test?

(A) After shampooing

(B) When hair is wet

(C) Extreme, uneven, or resistant porosity

(D) During scalp treatment

Q46. In this context what is the main cause of patches of alopecia that are erythematous and scaly requiring systemic treatment?

(A) Trichotillomania

(B) Tinea capitis

(C) Telogen effluvium

(D) Androgenetic alopecia

Q47. For the treatment of female pattern hair loss, which low level light therapy devices are FDA-cleared?

(A) Laser combs

(B) Infrared brushes

(C) UV scalp caps

(D) LED headbands

Q48. In primary cicatricial scarring alopecia, what is the main goal of treatment concerning symptoms like burning and tenderness?

(A) Hair regrowth

(B) Hyperkeratosis reduction

(C) Sebaceous gland stimulation

(D) Reducing underlying inflammation

Q49. In Central Centrifugal Cicatricial Alopecia, which layer of the scalp is affected as revealed by pathology, with findings including lymphocytic infiltrate and fibrosis?

(A) Epidermis

(B) Dermis

(C) Subcutaneous Tissue

(D) Sebaceous Glands

Q50. When should a patch test be conducted for treatments involving tinting the skin and hair?

(A) During the treatment

(B) At least 24 hours before

(C) After the treatment

(D) Monthly

Q51. To ensure the longevity of electrical tools like blow dryers and clippers, which of the following steps should a cosmetologist take?

A) Causes hair damage

B) Provides gentle and efficient drying

C) Ensures hygiene and safety

D) Regular cleaning and disinfection

Q52. Which distinctive feature makes hydraulic chair different from other cosmetology equipment?

(A) Aesthetically pleasing design

(B) Adjustable height for stylist comfort

(C) Advanced hair cutting features

(D) Cost-effectiveness

Q53. In cosmetology settings, what is the main objective of using electrical or electronic tools?

(A) Decorative styling

(B) Enhance curls

(C) Complete various services

(D) Minimize cleaning efforts

Q54. What is the importance of regular cleaning and disinfecting of salon workstation in cosmetology?

(A) Enhancing workstation aesthetics

(B) Minimizing salon costs

(C) Preventing contamination and infections

(D) Improving stylist comfort

Q55. From the following options, what is the role of using an all-purpose comb in cosmetology services?

(A) Sectioning hair for cutting

(B) Smoothing wavy ridges

(C) Creating curls

(D) Versatility in styling

Q56. What is the contribution of plastic bag to the hairstyling process in cosmetology?

(A) Adds shine to the hair

(B) Achieves closer cuts

(C) Wet hair styling

(D) Changes hair structure

Q57. In cosmetology settings, what is the importance of using different sizes of curling irons for creating versatile looks?

(A) Adds shine to the hair

(B) Precision cutting

(C) Enhances client comfort

(D) Provides versatility in curl sizes and patterns

Q58. Which of the following tools does cosmetologists commonly used for isolating specific hair sections?

(A) Hairpin

(B) Barber chair

(C) Hair roller

(D) Sectioning clip

Q59. For clients with delicate hair, what is the contribution of a microfiber towel in cosmetology services?

(A) Adds comfort to the client

(B) Enhances hair color absorption

(C) Ensures hygiene and safety

(D) Provides gentle and efficient drying

Q60. After a shampoo service in salon which type of towel is commonly used for blotting and drying hair?

(A) Microfiber towel

(B) Terry cloth towel

(C) Linen towel

(D) Thermal towel

Q61. During cutting, styling, and treating hair, how should a cosmetologist properly handle hair pins and clips?

(A) Wearing them on clothes for easy access

(B) Storing them in pockets for quick retrieval

(C) Using them to secure hair in place

(D) Keeping them clean and disinfected

Q62. In cosmetology services, what is the reason behind using a fuse in electrical equipment?

(A) Adds moisture to the hair

(B) Prevents excessive current and circuit overload

(C) Enhances hair color

(D) Improves hair texture

Q63. When it is recommended to refrain from massaging a client's scalp in the shampooing procedure?

(A) If a scalp condition is apparent

(B) After applying conditioner

(C) Only during chemical services

(D) If abrasions are present

Q64. Distinguishing it from other practices why is frequent conditioning emphasized for natural hair in cosmetology?

(A) Increase hair porosity

(B) Enhance scalp health

(C) Combat damage and maintain hair health

(D) Expedite chemical service application

Q65. What specific practice should be avoided for optimal client comfort to prevent tangling during a scalp massage?

(A) Scratching the scalp

(B) Using fingernails

(C) Applying consistent pressure

(D) Stroking the scalp sideways

Q66. Leading to the shedding of the skin cells, what skin condition results from the growth of masassezia?

(A) Tinea barbae

(B) Scabies

(C) Pediculous capitalis

(D) Dandruff

Q67. Ensuring optimal client experience, what specific function does a paper neck strip serve in the draping process?

(A) Enhance client comfort

(B) Absorb excess water

(C) Protect the neck from the cape's band

(D) Add a decorative touch

Q68. What specific aspect should stylists assess for optimal client care during the chemical draping procedure?

(A) Stylist's skills

(B) Hair color

(C) Dryness of towels

(D) Makeup application

Q69. What essential aspect should stylists thoroughly evaluate for optimal client care while conducting the chemical draping procedure?

(A) Stylist's skills

(B) Hair color

(C) Dryness of towels

(D) Makeup application

Q70. Due to potential breaking points in the strands, which hair type is the most prone to breakage?

(A) Type 1 - Straight

(B) Type 2 - Wavy

(C) Type 3 - Curly

(D) Type 4 - Coily/Kinky

Q71. When designing for different body shapes, what is the primary considerations?

(A) Hair color

(B) Face shape

(C) Body proportion

(D) Wave patterns

Q72. To achieve a fuller appearance, which hair type is best suited for diffusing?

(A) Straight, medium

(B) Wavy, fine

(C) Curly, medium

(D) Extremely curly, fine

Q73. In this context for a full haircut or to texturize specific areas for a softer effect, which tool is suitable?

(A) Haircutting shears

(B) Straight razors

(C) Texturizing shears

(D) Trimmers

Q74. Which of the following tools is traditionally replaced with liquid styling gels in the context of wet hairstyles

(A) Rollers

(B) Combs

(C) Waving lotion

(D) Brushes

Q75. On very curly hair, which of the following tools is used to create smooth and straight styles?

(A) Vent brush

(B) Metal comb

(C) Flat iron

(D) Wide-tooth comb

Q76. In the context of braiding, what is the main purpose of using small rubber bands or wires?

(A) Secure ends

(B) Add shine

(C) Detangle

(D) Create volume

Q77. To make a beautiful cornrows, which of the following option should be considered?

(A) Square partings

(B) Triangular partings

(C) Consistent partings

(D) Rectangular partings

Q78. In the context of cosmetology, what is the main difference between hair extensions and hairpieces?

(A) Attachment methods

(B) Length of wear

(C) Blending of real and artificial hair

(D) Use of Velcro

Q79. Which recommended practice regarding heat setting should be followed during ironing lightened & tinted or relaxed hair?

(A) Use maximum heat

(B) Avoid heat

(C) Use gentle heat

(D) Vary heat randomly

Q80. In a permanent waving what is the determining factor for the strength of the solution?

(A) Addition of oxygen

(B) Rebuilding disulfide bonds

(C) Removal of hydrogen

(D) Deactivating waving solution

Q81. In the texture or movement of hair, which layer is not directly involved?

(A) Cortex

(B) Medulla

(C) Cuticle

(D) Epidermis

Q82. In general, what procedures are employed to test hair porosity?

(A) Observe shine

(B) Conduct a strand test

(C) Perform a scalp massage

(D) Analyze hair density

Q83. In hair treatment, which method involves the direct application of lightener to styled, clean hair?

(A) Foil technique

(B) Cap technique

(C) Baliage technique

(D) Free-form technique

Q84. Which relaxer variant that used in drain cleaners both the oldest and most widely used?

(A) No-Lye relaxers

(B) Lye-based relaxers

(C) Metal hydroxide relaxers

(D) Thio relaxers

Q85. In permanent waving, what is the determining factor for the strength of the solution?

(A) Processing time

(B) Hair thickness

(C) Rod size

(D) Reducing agent concentration

Q86. In a permanent wave, when does most processing occur?

(A) After 15 minutes

(B) Within the first 5-10 minutes

(C) After 30 minutes

(D) Before applying the solution

Q87. How can we describe the features of hair that is wavy?

(A) Tight curls

(B) No waves or curls

(C) Gentle waves

(D) Dense coils

Q88. What type of hair is the most delicate and demands meticulous care?

(A) Straight Hair

(B) Wavy Hair

(C) Curly Hair

(D) Coily/Kinky Hair

Q89. When providing facial treatments, why is maintaining a serene environment important?

(A) Boost retail revenue

(B) Guarantee client tranquility

(C) Maximize salon profits

(D) Streamline treatment efficiency

Q90. Considering the following options, what does dry skin tend to feel especially after cleansing?

(A) Oily

(B) Tight

(C) Cool

(D) Smooth

Q91. Before doing beauty treatments, which skin condition may require a medical note?

(A) Minor rashes

(B) Recent bruising

(C) Dry skin

(D) Fine lines

Q92. When using Water Hydrogel Eye patches with other skincare products, what precaution is necessary?

(A) Apply under-eye patches with intense treatments

(B) Use eye patches with any serum or cream

(C) Wash the face immediately after removing the patch

(D) Reuse the under eye patches for multiple applications

Q93. In the context of dermal application, which skincare product category includes gel, lotions, and creams?

(A) Anti-aging products

(B) Sunbathing products

(C) Emollients

(D) Anti-acne products

Q94. Considering the following options, what is the purpose of a Material Safety Data Sheet (MSDS) in a saloon?

(A) Hair styling

(B) Skin hydration

(C) Hazard information

(D) Nail coloration

Q95. Considering the given options, how can cosmetologists reduce the risk of musculoskeletal disorders like tunnel syndrome?

(A) Use heavier tools

(B) Ignore body posture

(C) Hold implements tightly

(D) Practice ergonomic principles

Q96. From the given option, what is the skin condition that requires avoiding harsh or stimulating treatments?

(A) Eczema

(B) Psoriasis

(C) Lupus

(D) Acne

Q97. While performing temporary hair removal, what is the main purpose of applying depilatory?

(A) Softening the hair

(B) Removing hair from the follicle

(C) Dissolving hair at the skin surface

(D) Destroying hair growth cells

Q98. In the context of makeup application, how does the cosmetologist imagine the client's facial appearance?

(A) A blank canvas

(B) A colorful palette

(C) A predefined template

(D) A natural landscape

Q99. In the context skin care, what are the main objectives of iontophoresis?

(A) Creating bold color combinations

(B) Stimulating blood flow

(C) Penetrating water-soluble products

(D) Enhancing natural skin tone

Q100. In the context of future salon visits, what is the importance of client documentation?

(A) Assisting in sales promotion

(B) Supporting service standardization

(C) Managing salon expenses

(D) Optimizing salon layout

Q101. During a client consultation, which of the following factor should be considered while determining the nail plate's shape and length?

(A) Hair texture

(B) Facial symmetry

(C) Type of nail polish

(D) Hand shape and cuticle area

Q102. Considering the following option, which nail condition would possibly restrict but not necessarily prohibit a service?

(A) Onychophagy

(B) Broken bones

(C) Paronychia

(D) Onychomadesis

Q103. If a client is looking to add length and durability to their nails, which product or service would be most appropriate for him?

(A) Nail wraps

(B) Acrylic nail extensions

(C) Nail art stamping

(D) Cuticle oil treatment

Q104. For a cosmetologist, what is the importance of maintaining accurate records of products utilized during services?

(A) To track salon equipment maintenance

(B) To comply with salon inventory audits

(C) To provide transparency to clients

(D) To monitor salon marketing campaigns

Q105. To equalize the porosity of the hair in nail care which of the following tool is specifically used?

(A) Shampoo

(B) Fillers

(C) Lightener

(D) Developer

Q106. During a manicure, why it is important to use nail files with lower grit with caution?

(A) Enhances nail thickness

(B) Causes excessive thinning

(C) Improves surface smoothness

(D) Facilitates cuticle removal

Q107. From the following options, before placing implements in the disinfectant solution, what is the crucial step?

(A) Rinse and air dry

(B) Sterilize

(C) Wipe with a damp cloth

(D) Sanitize and disinfect

Q108. As suggested by the cosmetologists, how nail technicians can accommodate clients to mitigate potential ergonomic issues?

(A) Ignoring client comfort

(B) Adapting to clients' needs

(C) Using heavy nail equipment

(D) Increasing appointment duration

Q109. From the following options, before applying polish why it is important to remove all traces of lotion or oil from the nail plate?

(A) Improves adhesion

(B) Adds shine

(C) Enhances color

(D) Speeds up drying

Q110. What should be avoided to prevent product discoloration during acrylic nail enhancement?

(A) Applying nail dehydrator

(B) Using wet primer

(C) Buffing with high-shine buffer

(D) Applying enhancement over existing polish

Test 4 Answer key

Q1.

Answer: C

Explanation: To avoid potential harm and legal responsibility, Infection prevention is vital in cosmetology. Please note that, it is also necessary to fulfill legal obligations.

Q2.

Answer: D

Explanation: Bacteria enter the body through broken skin or other entry points. In salons, pathogenic bacteria are the main cause of infection.

Q3.

Answer: C

Explanation: In barbering, to ensure equipment safety and hygiene. The most effective technique for preventing, HIV transmission is standardized disinfection and sterilisation.

Q4.

Answer: C

Explanation: In the salon setting, disinfection eradicates many or all pathogenic microorganisms, to ensure client safety and hygiene.

Q5.

Answer: A

Explanation: It is advised to encase, cosmetology implements in an airtight container. To enhance safety, after disinfection.

Q6.

Answer: B

Explanation: In cosmetology, chelating detergent is used for foot spa cleaning. Please note that, chelating detergent removes visible debris from surfaces.

Q7.

Answer: D

Explanation: The transfer of microorganisms can be prevented via proper sanitation of tools. Consequently, this process reduces cross contamination between clients.

Q8.

Answer: B

Explanation: The transmission of microorganisms can occur due to the handling of contaminated towels. As a result, the handling of contaminated towels can contribute to cross-contamination risks.

Q9.

Answer: D

Explanation: Please note that, federal law, emphasizes the importance of adherence to product usage guidelines in a salon. Failure to follow instructions violates federal law.

Q10.

Answer: D

Explanation: As the main role of the EPA is to license disinfectants, in cosmetology. Besides this, it can also establish rules for the environmental impact of salon practices.

Q11.

Answer: B

Explanation: To enhance workplace safety, MSDS, provides critical details on salon product handling. Please note that, it also ensures the practitioner is following safe procedures.

Q12.

Answer: C

Explanation: In case of a practitioner's injury, to ensure complete decontamination and safety in the salon setting. The first step is to double-bagged contaminated objects. Next, must prioritize cleaning affected surfaces and implements.

Q13.

Answer: C

Explanation: To remove visible debris from salon tools and equipment. In the cleaning process, an ultrasonic can be utilized.

Q14.

Answer: B

Explanation: In case of a blood exposure injury, to reduce the danger of infection an aseptic technique can be used. An aseptic technique can also be used to ensure proper wound care.

Q15.

Answer: A

Explanation: The hair bulb contains the dermal papilla, which is essential for providing nutrients for hair growth.

Q16.

Answer: B

Explanation: Sweat glands excrete perspiration, which helps in the regulation of temperature through evaporative cooling.

Q17.

Answer: A

Explanation: The hyponychium is present below the nail's free edge, which acts as a protective barrier. It also protects against foreign substances between the nail plate and living skin.

Q18.

Answer: B

Explanation: Seborrheic dermatitis is a scalp condition, which involves oily scales, redness, itching, and yellowish scales.

Q19.

Answer: B

Explanation: Contact dermatitis causes hair loss due to an allergic reaction to particular hair products.

Q20.

Answer: A

Explanation: Exfoliation helps in the removal of dead skin cells, and can prevent pore blockage and skin problems like blackheads and pimples.

Q21.

Answer: A

Explanation: Discolored nails are the term that is used for changed colors of nails, due to systemic issues or circulation problems.

Q22.

Answer: C

Explanation: The auriculotemporal nerve is the nerve that affects the skin above the temple to the top of the skull.

Q23.

Answer: A

Explanation: Neuron is the fundamental structural unit of the nervous system.

Q24.

Answer: C

Explanation: The autonomic nervous system is responsible for the management of involuntary muscle activities.

Q25.

Answer: C

Explanation: Blood circulation affects the rate of nail growth. It can impact the actual growth process of nails.

Q26.

Answer: D

Explanation: The knowledge of blood circulation helps in minimizing the risks of chemical treatments.

Q27.

Answer: B

Explanation: Understanding foot anatomy is essential in cosmetology. The foot is made up of 26 bones.

Q28.

Answer: A

Explanation: The femur and pelvic bone (pelvis) combine to form the hip joint. In cosmetology, understanding hip anatomy is important.

Q29.

Answer: D

Explanation: The water droplets are internal due to the external oil portion, making the emulsion feel greasier in water-in-oil emulsions.

Q30.

Answer: B

Explanation: By forming a protective layer on the hair shaft, Silicones function as water-resistant lubricants, contributing to enhanced shine in hair products.

Q31.

Answer: A

Explanation: In hair color and nail enhancements oxidation reactions are exothermic, releasing heat. For safe and effective service cosmetologists should comprehend these changes.

Q32.

Answer: B

Explanation: the combined properties of substances included in a physical mixture determines the properties of it. For product understanding and application cosmetologists need this knowledge.

Q33.

Answer: D

Explanation: During the bleaching process, causing a color transformation, Hydrogen peroxide changes hair color by oxidizing melanin.

Q34.

Answer: D

Explanation: In the context of permanently changing hair shape, permanent waves reshape hair by reducing di-sulfur bonds. This reduction process defines the perm's lasting effect, making the hair structurally flexible.

Q35.

Answer: C

Explanation: Please note that constant opening and closing of the cuticle can lead long hair to irreparable damage due to soap-based products.

Q36.

Answer: A

Explanation: Due to its accuracy and consistency in pH readings, a person could choose a pH meter as it offers a longer lifespan and precision.

Q37.

Answer: C

Explanation: In the context of nail care products, toluene is utilized to dissolve substances. For smoother application and lasting results, it facilitate the formulation of nail polishes and related cosmetics.

Q38.

Answer: C

Explanation: By introducing a reducing agent to break down and reshape hair bonds, permanent waves chemically change the structure of hair permanently.

Q39.

Answer: B

Explanation: If a client's desired color goal goes beyond the safe lifting capacity, find a compromise or adjust the long-term plan, strand tests can guide decisions.

Q40.

Answer: B

Explanation: During the use of bleach, strand tests play a crucial role in revealing if hair lifts and helping choose the right product and anticipate underlying pigments exposed.

Q41.

Answer: D

Explanation: Being a good listener during the client consultation builds strong relationships between clients and cosmetologists, which is essential for client satisfaction and retention in the cosmetology profession.

Q42.

Answer: B

Explanation: Salicylic acid, effectively treats pomade scalp acne by unclogging pores and reducing small bumps and comedowns near the hairline.

Q43.

Answer: C

Explanation: In dealing with relative contraindication, it is important for modifying the treatment and providing approval, ensuring client safety under professional guidance.

Q44.

Answer: A

Explanation: To prioritize client safety, it is essential for a cosmetologist to delay treatment when a client has undiagnosed facial lumps or swelling.

Q45.

Answer: C

Explanation: Dealing with extreme, uneven, or resistant porosity, it is important to utilize strand tests to ensure the desired result and avoid poor outcomes.

Q46.

Answer: B

Explanation: The main cause of patches of alopecia is Tinea capitis which presents as erythematous and scaly, necessitating systemic treatment.

Q47.

Answer: A

Explanation: For treating female pattern hair loss, low-level light therapy devices such as laser combs are FDA- cleared.

Q48.

Answer: D

Explanation: It is the treatment goal for primary cicatricial scarring alopecia to reduce the underlying inflammation and associated symptoms.

Q49.

Answer: B

Explanation: In Central Centrifugal Cicatricial Alopecia, pathological findings include lymphocytic infiltrate and fibrosis in the dermal layer.

Q50.

Answer: B

Explanation: For tinting treatments, conduct patch tests at least 24 hours before the actual treatment.

Q51.

Answer: D

Explanation: In cosmetology practices, regular cleaning and disinfection contribute to the longevity of electrical tools, maintaining hygiene and safety.

Q52.

Answer: B

Explanation: Hydraulic chairs are known for their adjustable height. They provide flexibility and comfort for stylists during various salon services.

Q53.

Answer: C

Explanation: In cosmetology settings electrical tools are used for various purposes, allowing a diverse array of services.

Q54.

Answer: C

Explanation: In cosmetology it is necessary to regularly clean and disinfect salon work station to prevent contamination and infection control. It ensures a safe environment for clients.

Q55.

Answer: D

Explanation: Cosmetologists use an all- purpose comb in styling various hair types because it can be used in many ways.

Q56.

Answer: C

Explanation: Plastic bags help to retain moisture and achieve specific styling effects. Cosmetologists use plastic bags to cover the hair during wet styling.

Q57.

Answer: D

Explanation: The use of different sizes of curling irons provides versatility in curl sizes and patterns, which helps cosmetologists create a wide range of looks.

Q58.

Answer: D

Explanation: In cosmetology, sectioning clips are commonly used for isolating specific hair sections during cutting, coloring, or styling processes in cosmetology.

Q59.

Answer: D

Explanation: In cosmetology services, microfiber towels provide gentle and efficient drying, making them suitable for clients with delicate hair.

Q60.

Answer: B

Explanation: After a shampoo service in salon, cosmetologists commonly use terry cloth towels for blotting and drying hair.

Q61.

Answer: D

Explanation: During hair cutting, styling, and treatment process, hair pins and clips should be kept clean and disinfected to prevent contamination.

Q62.

Answer: B

Explanation: Using a fuse in electrical equipment prevents excessive current and circuit overload, and also ensures safety in the salon.

Q63.

Answer: D

Explanation: To prevent discomfort or irritation, it is recommended to avoid scalp massage if abrasions are present on the client's scalp.

Q64.

Answer: C

Explanation: To actively combat damage and sustain the overall health of natural hair, regular conditioning serves as a key strategy in cosmetology.

Q65.

Answer: B

Explanation: Ensuring a smooth and comfortable experience for the client, it is advisable to avoid using fingernails during a scalp massage to prevent tangling.

Q66.

Answer: D

Explanation: Prompting the shedding of skin cells on the scalp, the occurrence of dandruff is attributed to the proliferation of masassezia.

Q67.

Answer: C

Explanation: During draping the main purpose of a paper neck strip is to shield the neck from potential discomfort caused by the cape's band.

Q68.

Answer: C

Explanation: Stylists should diligently check the dryness of towels and promptly replace them if needed to ensure client comfort, during chemical draping process.

Q69.

Answer: C

Explanation: During the chemical draping process it is important to ensure the dryness of towels and promptly replace them if necessary.

Q70.

Answer: D

Explanation: Due tight coils in its structure, Type 4 coily/kinky hair is notably prone to breakage.

Q71.

Answer: C

Explanation: In this context, when designing for different body shapes, consider the client's body shape to avoid styles that appear out of proportion.

Q72.

Answer: B

Explanation: Please note that, wavy, fine hair is best suited for diffusing as it responds well for a fuller look. But caution is needed to avoid damage.

Q73.

Answer: B

Explanation: In this context, a straight razor is used for a full haircut or texturing. It is also employed for a softening effect on the ends of the hair.

Q74.

Answer: C

Explanation: Waving lotions are traditionally replaced with liquid styling gels in the context of wet hairstyles. Traditionally, karaya gum based lotions are often used for shaping hair

Q75.

Answer: C

Explanation: On very curly hair, flat irons with straight edges are used to create smooth and straight styles. These versatile tools are used for achieving diverse looks.

Q76.

Answer: A

Explanation: In the braiding context. Small rubber bands or wires ensure a neat and secure finish for different styles. They play an important role in braiding by securing the ends of the braids.

Q77.

Answer: C

Explanation: The beauty of cornrows depends on a consistent, even separation. Which provides a solid foundation for braiding techniques.

Q78.

Answer: B

Explanation: In the context of cosmetology, hair is left in the hair for a long time. And unlike a piece of hair, it is not removed at night.

Q79.

Answer: C

Explanation: In this context, to maintain the health of the hair during styling. It is recommended to use gentle heat for lightened & tinted or relaxed hair to avoid damage.

Q80.

Answer: B

Explanation: Thio neutralization rebuilds hair bonds broken during waving solution application.

Q81.

Answer: C

Explanation: The cuticle though protective is not directly involved in texture or movement.

Q82.

Answer: B

Explanation: Hair porosity is tested by taking strands from various areas & assessing their feel.

Q83.

Answer: C

Explanation: Baliage involves painting lightener directly onto the hair for subtle effects.

Q84.

Answer: B

Explanation: Lye-based relaxers common and oldest, share chemistry with drain cleaners.

Q85.

Answer: D

Explanation: The strength is based on the concentration of the reducing agent.

Q86.

Answer: B

Explanation: Processing peaks within the initial 5-10 minutes.

Q87.

Answer: C

Explanation: Wavy hair falls between straight & curly with gentle waves.

Q88.

Answer: D

Explanation: Coily/kinky hair has tight, dense curls & needs delicate care.

Q89.

Answer: B

Explanation: In order to guarantee client tranquility, maintain a serene environment is vital during facial treatments. Please note that this focus on relaxation fostering client satisfaction and loyalty, enhances the overall experiences.

Q90.

Answer: B

Explanation: Please note that after performing cleansing dry skin tends to feel tight, indicating potential for flakiness and lack of moistures.

Q91.

Answer: B

Explanation: Please note that, recent bruising may require a medical note because it poses a risk of infections, and medial note ensures safety of beauty treatment.

Q92.

Answer: A

Explanation: While performing severe treatments like Clay Masks, retinol, and AHAs apply under-eye patches to enhance efficacy and please avoid potential interference with other products.

Q93.

Answer: C

Explanation: Please note that gels, creams, oils, and lotions collectively known as emollients, are created for dermal application, they enhance skin softness and nourishment.

Q94.

Answer: C

Explanation: Material Safety Data Sheet ensure salon professionals understand and reduce risks associated with the use of salon products, and also serves to provide necessary hazard information.

Q95.

Answer: D

Explanation: Cosmetologists can prevent musculoskeletal disorders like carpal tunnel syndrome by practicing ergonomic principles, including utilizing proper tools and maintaining good body postures.

Q96.

Answer: C

Explanation: In order to prevent worsening of the condition, clients with lupus should avoid harsh or stimulating treatments.

Q97.

Answer: C

Explanation: The main purpose of applying depilatory is to dissolve hair at the skin surface. This makes it a temporary method of hair removal.

Q98.

Answer: A

Explanation: In the context of makeup application, cosmetologists imagine the client's face as a blank canvas to creatively apply skills, allowing for artistic and personalized expression.

Q99.

Answer: C

Explanation: Please note that the main objectives of iontophoresis is using galvanic current to penetrate water-soluble products into the skin, optimizing the impact of skincare treatments.

Q100.

Answer: B

Explanation: During salon visits, client documentation supports service standardization by facilitating personalized and consistent experiences.

Q101.

Answer: D

Explanation: In the nail care process, hand shape and cuticle area should influence the ideal shape and length of the nail plate. It enhances the overall fingertip appearance.

Q102.

Answer: A

Explanation: While onychiphagy might restrict a service, conditions like broken bones, paronychia and onychomadesis could potentially prevent a service.

Q103.

Answer: B

Explanation: When a client looking to provide both length and durability of nails, please note that acrylic nail extensions are the most appropriate option.

Q104.

Answer: C

Explanation: To provide transparency to clients, it is essential to maintain accurate records of products used during services.

Q105.

Answer. B

Explanation: In the view of above, in nail care fillers are used to equalize hair porosity.

Q106.

Answer. B

Explanation: During the use of lower grit abrasive files caution is required, as they are aggressive and can cause excessive thinning and damage to the natural nail.

Q107.

Answer. A

Explanation: For ensuring proper hygiene, before implements in the disinfectant solution, they must be rinsed and air-dried.

Q108.

Answer. B

Explanation: By adopting to clients' needs nail technicians can mitigate potential ergonomic issues, as recommended by the cosmetologists.

Q109.

Answer. A

Explanation: Please note that, to make sure proper adhesion of the polish to the nail plate complete removal of oil or lotion.

Q110.

Answer. B

Explanation: For preventing product discoloration in acrylic nail procedures, it is avoided to applying enhancement over wet primer.

Reward / Bonous

Reward Worth is $120, Get this by scanning QR

1. **Reward** – Complete Audio book of 4 PTS
2. **Reward** – Complete 3 Extra PTS of Comes logy Exam
3. **Reward** – Complete Audio Book of 3 Extra PTS of Comes logy Exam
4. **Reward** – Flash Card in Anki App
5. **Reward** – Complete Study Guide of How To Overcome From Exam
6. **Reward** – Audio File Of How To Overcome From Exam Stress.

Scan Below to get this Reward